WITHOUT RETURN

WITHOUT RETURN

Memoirs of an Egyptian Jew 1930-1957

Jacques Sardas

Thebes Press
Dallas

Published by Thebes Press
Dallas, Texas

The frontispiece shows the corniche, or coastal boulevard, in Alexandria circa 1935 (photo courtesy of the Library of Congress); all other photographs are from the Sardas family collection.

The Thebes Press logo is adapted from a photograph
of Black-figure Amphora
Attributed to the Phineas Painter
South Italian or Greek, "Chalcidian" (probably made in Rhegium [modern Reggio Calabria], South Italy),
ca. 520–510 BCE
Ceramic
Tampa Museum of Art, Joseph Veach Noble Collection, purchased in part with funds donated by Florida Steel Corporation 1986.013

Book design by Patrice Sheridan

Printed in the United States of America

ISBN 978-0-9980849-0-9

For my mother, Dora Beja Sardas,
who sacrificed her life for her children

For Etty, my wife,
to whom I owe everything

And for my grandchildren and future generations,
so they will know our story and be inspired to tell their own

CONTENTS

PREFACE

When my grandson Jake was around fifteen years old, he and I decided to share brunch every weekend. Like many teenagers, he was struggling with timeless questions about God, death, and the meaning of life. During our brunches he shared his thoughts on politics and worldwide conflicts with passionate concern. I assured him that at his age, I had similar questions—except he was far more knowledgeable and intelligent than I was at his age. I described to him my difficult childhood, my hesitations and doubts, and I told him that I nonetheless found life beautiful and meaningful while I was growing up. Much to my surprise Jake proved to be sincerely interested in my stories. He would stare at me and exclaim, "Cool! Cool, go on . . ."

One day Jake asked, "Why don't you write a book?" When I told him that I was not good at writing and that there was no way I would write any book, especially not a book about my life, Jake insisted: "It's for us, not for you. It would be great to have it for our family."

That made me stop to think. Jake was asking me to write the book not for myself but for my family and future generations. Maybe he was right. When Jake noticed that my resistance was fading, he put his hand on my shoulder, the way I usually do whenever I give him advice. "Jacky," he said, "you always tell us that determination is the key to success."

I smiled. How could I refuse? "I'll do my best," I said.

* * *

The title of this book, *Without Return*, comes from the words that were stamped on my passport in 1957, when I was preparing to leave Egypt. Nationalist sentiment at the time was high: anti-Semitic rhetoric was everywhere, and persecution of Jews and people of European descent was on the rise. With the Greek passport that had been obtained with difficulty by my father, I got my exit visa from the Egyptian authorities only a few days before my trip. When at last I was able to look at it, I saw that below the visa stamp there was a handwritten note in Arabic: *Moughadra nihaëya bedoun awda*: "Departure definitive, without return." Good riddance, the authorities seemed to be saying. We don't want you back.

It occurred to me then that I would never be able to return to the country I had called home for twenty-six years. Those days were over. It was up to me now: there was no going back. The best I could do was remember—and remember well.

Fortunately, many memories came to mind as I sat down to write. At times I couldn't decide what to put in the book and what to leave out. After all, over the course of eighty-six years, I have experienced difficult moments, scary moments, and challenging moments as well as happy, joyful, and rewarding moments. Many of them are related with candor in the pages that follow. So if you are interested in the story of a Jewish boy born in Egypt, how he discovered who he was and what he was meant to live for; if you want to experience his pains, tackle his doubts, endure his anxieties, and relish his joys—then follow me.

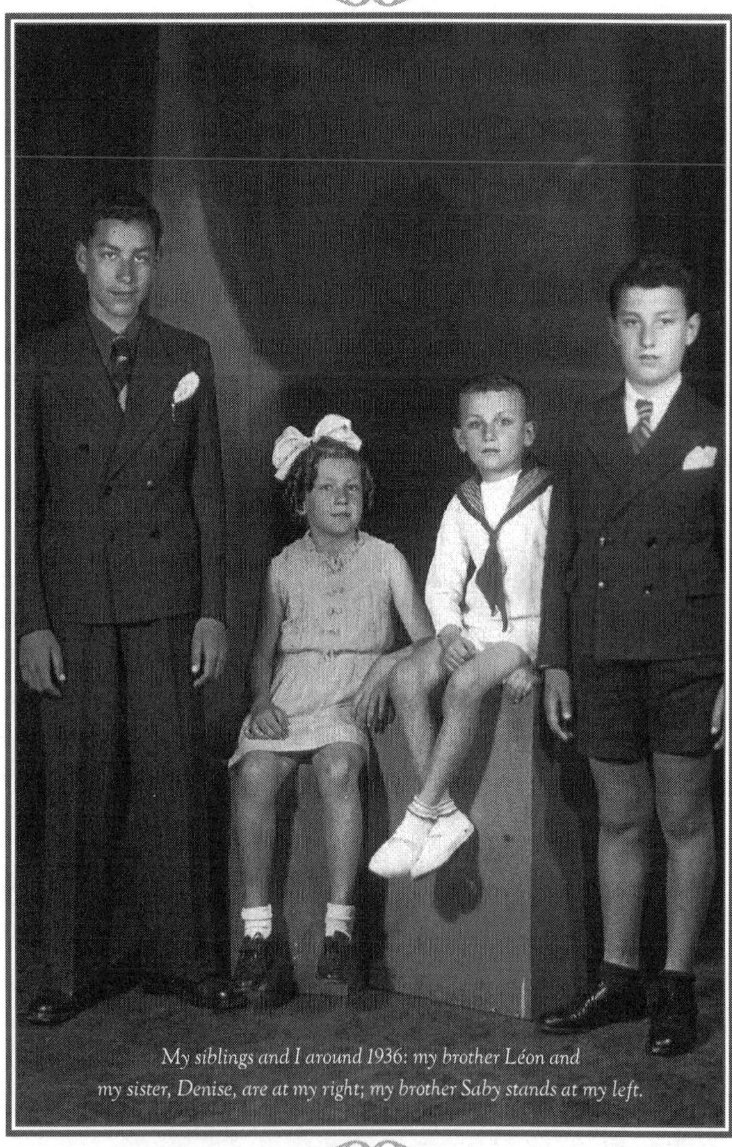

My siblings and I around 1936: my brother Léon and my sister, Denise, are at my right; my brother Saby stands at my left.

CHAPTER 1

IN MY EARLIEST recollection I am four, and we are living in a small two-story house in Alexandria. My mother holds a large tray of food and cautiously tries to navigate her way through a crowd of noisy people that fills our house. This was quite an unusual event: we seldom had visitors and never in such large numbers. Even more unusual was serving the visitors food. I remember sitting at the bottom of the stairs and eating a sugar cookie—also an extraordinary event. I rested my chin on my knees, smiled, and stared with my large green eyes at all those strangers. The special occasion was a shiva, a religious period of mourning, for my paternal grandfather, Léon Sardas, who had just died after a long illness.

Our house was located on Kenya Street in Ibrahimieh, a suburb of Alexandria that was home to a large Greek community. The majority of the Egyptian Arabs working in Ibrahimieh spoke Greek. Several Greek families who had lived there for many years could not speak any language but their own—and they had no need to. Walking along the main streets of Ibrahimieh, visitors might think they were in Athens. The coffee shops had sidewalk tables where men sipped their Greek coffee and gesticulated as they played *tavli*, or backgammon. French was Egypt's diplomatic, judicial, and official language, a vestige of the Napoleonic era. Most of the highly educated Egyptians, as well as foreigners in Egypt, spoke French and attended French schools. More street signs were written in French than in Arabic.

In our small backyard Dad had a henhouse just like the one his family had during his childhood in the Cretan city of Chania. The hens provided fresh eggs and occasional meals. One night my father heard a strange sound. Intrigued, he opened the window and saw a hen sticking her neck out of the henhouse and crowing. Crowing at night was already a bad sign, but crowing by a hen was definitely a bad omen. He took a big kitchen knife, went to the backyard, and, because he did not know which hen had crowed, slaughtered them all, thereby saving us from the evil that would otherwise have struck us. The next morning Mom explained the immense financial and emotional sacrifice our father had made to protect us. She then looked at us with a resigned smile and affirmed, in a mixture of Hebrew and Greek, that he did it *kappara yassas* ("for your salvation's sake"). I believe that this event was the main reason my parents decided to move to another house, also in Ibrahimieh, shortly thereafter.

* * *

My parents' ancestors were Sephardic Jews, originally from Spain. They endured persecution during the Spanish

Inquisition. Most Jews fled Spain to avoid torture, death, or conversion to Christianity. They immigrated to less hostile refuges in other countries, particularly Turkey. At that time Turkey was the center of the Ottoman Empire, which stretched from Europe to Africa. The Ottomans opened their doors to the fugitive Jews because they brought adaptability, knowledge of languages, trade, and craft, and much-needed economic stability. The Ottomans, in exchange, provided the Jews with a secure environment, freedom, and religious tolerance. They developed their own language, Judeo-Español, also called Ladino, a mixture of Spanish and Hebrew. My parents spoke Ladino but did not teach it to us. Perhaps they were caught up in the day-to-day struggle of making ends meet and looking after four children, or maybe they did not want us to understand their conversations. They told us little about our family history, but we knew that their grandparents and great-grandparents had lived in Izmir, a pleasant city and a major Turkish port on the Aegean Sea.

Although my father claimed that he was born in Crete, we do not know for sure. He certainly was raised there and acquired the Cretan accent as well as the Cretans' impetuous character. My father used to mix truth and fiction to make his exploits more exciting, particularly his war stories. When it was time for bed, we always awaited his stories with eager anticipation. In the darkness they took on such mythical proportions that we believed every epic adventure he related.

My father, Raphael, and his younger brother, Vita, short for Vitali, were born to Léon Sardas and his wife, Doudou. We never found out if this was her real name; everyone just called her Doudou. We also do not know her maiden name.

Léon and Doudou divorced early in my father's life; she left Léon because he was a womanizer and had many affairs. We never found out exactly what Grandpa Léon did for a living, but he seems to have had a business in Chania involving olive oil, wine, and grains.

My mother, Dora, was born to Shabetay Beja and his wife, Mazeltov Mordo. Shabetay and Mazeltov had eight children—seven girls and one boy: Behora, Maurice, Zimbul (also known as Morosa), Louise, Dora, Sarah, Mary, and Clarisse. My mother, the fifth child, always referred to her brother with respect and admiration. Her father, Shabetay,

My maternal grandparents, Shabetay and Mazeltov Mordo Beja

My mother's family, the Bejas, in the early 1920s; Dora sits at the far left

made a comfortable living from his pawn shop in Izmir. We assume that the Bejas lived there until World War I; after the war they immigrated to Europe and South America. Maurice left Izmir first, to complete his studies and find a job in Europe. He later worked in Spain as a director of the B. F. Goodrich tire company and then established his own business in Marseille. When she left Turkey, my mother—who had studied in Izmir until she was about thirteen or fourteen—went to France, where she continued her studies in English and French and later worked as a teacher. She met my father in Marseille and married him a few months later.

My parents, Dora and Raphael Sardas, around 1920, before their marriage

Their civil wedding took place in January of 1923 at Marseille's town hall.

In their *ketoubah*, the Jewish wedding contract, my father declared he was an interpreter. We suspect he was not actually employed. But as an adventurer, he could well have worked as an interpreter. His formal education probably never went beyond elementary school; nevertheless, he could speak more than ten languages. He was a handsome man, and my mother, twelve years younger, fell madly in love with him, to the dismay of her family. They, like many Jewish families, hoped that, with her education, she would marry a doctor, a lawyer, or an engineer who could offer her a secure future.

My mother and father in 1923

My mother's brother, Maurice, who was about my father's age, was at the time a wholesaler of grains, sugar, and flour in Marseille. He had married a woman named Ernestine Durin, and they had a son, René. Years later Maurice and Ernestine divorced; during World War II Maurice married Odette Deleuil, a Catholic woman. They had two children, Robert and Mathilde.

My father harbored an obsessive resentment against my mother's family, the Bejas. Although he never mentioned the reason to us, we suspected that he held a grudge against them because neither Uncle Maurice nor anyone else in my mother's family had offered my parents any financial help when they married. As time passed and life got tougher, his anger toward my mother's family only grew stronger, and he blamed them for all his financial misfortunes. My father's resentment lasted his whole life. He never forgot it and made sure that my mother did not forget it, either.

With no help or prospects in Marseille, my parents decided to move to Egypt, where my father's brother, Vita, had emigrated a few years earlier. My mother's dowry was just enough for the newlyweds to pay for their passage on a ship to Barcelona and from there to Alexandria, where they arrived early in 1923, a few months after their wedding. They had four children: Léon, born in 1923; Saby, who arrived in 1926; Denise, born in 1928; and me, Jacob, in 1930.

My uncle Vita had already started his own business in Alexandria, and my father hoped they would strike it rich together. My father was a tall, handsome, strong man—untamable and temperamental. His voice dominated any conversation, and his presence filled any room. Uncle Vita, on the other hand, was about five feet tall. Poised, organized, and disciplined, he had more education than my father had. Uncle Vita was quiet, calm, and extremely kind. His business involved imports and exports of various products, such as grains, coal, threads, and lubrication oil for machines. The business did so well for a while that Uncle Vita even owned a car, a rare luxury in Egypt at the time. Uncle Vita's wife, Pauline Cohen, who was born in Chania, had come to Egypt with her uncle, who served as the Italian consul in Crete. During that visit she met Vita and married him in 1929.

Prosperity, alas, did not last long. At the start of the Great Depression, Uncle Vita had to close his business. After a few months he obtained a good job at a Greek company, Tavoularides, a well-known and long-established firm that specialized in the same imports and exports as my uncle's old company had.

Vita and Pauline had a daughter in June of 1930, three months before I was born. They named her Denise, the same name as my sister, who had been born two years earlier. Both brothers were following a tradition of the time by naming their daughters after their own mothers. The first child was named for the paternal grandparent of the same sex, and the second child was named for the maternal grandparent of the same sex. Since she did not particularly like the sound of my grandmother's name, Doudou, my mother

My parents with (from left) Saby, me, Denisica, Denise, and Léon in 1932

persuaded my father to name my sister Denise. The letter *D* satisfied my father, and the French connotation pleased my mother. To differentiate between the two Denises, we called my cousin Denisica ("the small Denise"), and my sister was known as Denise. Uncle Vita and his family lived in an apartment building in Ibrahimieh about a mile from our house. Some of their Chania relatives, with whom they were very close, lived in the same building. This made life easier for Aunt Pauline. Uncle Vita and his family had a comfortable life. The story for my father was quite different.

* * *

My father was tough, but beneath his explosive character he hid a golden heart. He loved us and suffered most of his life because he could not provide the level of comfort he desired for the family. Despite his financial struggles, every year without fail, during the days preceding Yom Kippur, the Jewish day of atonement, my father managed to buy three roosters and a hen. He then offered them to poorer Jewish families as a *kappara*, an offering, in this case a rooster for each son and a hen for Denise. The rabbi who slaughtered them marked our foreheads with their blood, and all day our dad forbade us to wash it off. That way, he was certain the rite would protect us.

After several desperate months in Egypt without a job in the late 1920s, my father finally got work as a sales clerk in a store owned by a Greek. One day, after Dad had closed an important sale, he rewarded himself by lighting a Coutarelli, a strong Egyptian cigarette. His boss rushed up to him and said: "What do you think you're doing? You're not on vacation here—you can't smoke! Do you understand?" My father was shocked because he thought his boss would congratulate him for his performance. Dad grabbed the man so tightly by the throat that he was choking. With his thunderous voice, my father yelled in his ear, "Don't you ever, ever talk to me this way, *vre psoriari!*" ("you scabby scoundrel"). He left work, headed to a bar, and drank a couple of ouzos. He was still cursing in Greek when he got home.

My father never worked for anyone again. After several tries and many months of misery, he finally found work that did not compromise his pride and independence. He sold cloth for men's suits. Dad managed to find Greek and Turkish merchants who allowed him to take cloth on consignment. He then carried the fabrics in a suitcase, visited professional men in their offices, and persuaded them to buy his suit fabric. His targets were doctors, engineers, and bankers.

Most of his prospective clients were foreign-born, and he gained their confidence by literally speaking their language. He entered an office, looked around, and chose his prospect by the man's appearance. My father would guess the man's country of origin and start a conversation with him in his native tongue. Then my father would open his suitcase, remove fabric, and with a majestic and theatrical gesture place it carefully on the client's shoulder. He even had a few ties in his suitcase that matched the fabrics. Sometimes it worked, but more often it did not.

My father soon realized that he had to offer a greater selection of materials. He then packed two suitcases and hired an Arab, Abdul Meguid, to carry the heavier suitcase. Carrying his suitcase had given Dad huge right biceps. They

My father and Abdul Meguid

were about the size of a large orange and three or four times larger than the biceps on his left arm.

And I liked Abdul Meguid. Despite his physically demanding job, he smiled all the time, even while carrying the heavy suitcase. He proved exceptionally patient, always displayed good humor, and remained extremely loyal to my father. When Dad started his sales pitch, Abdul Meguid stood behind him, smiling and admiring my father's performance. The job proved physically and mentally exhausting. They started at about eight in the morning and did not finish before seven or eight at night.

When my father had money, he gave my mother enough to prepare dinner for that particular evening. Most of the time he had no money, and we waited for him to bring home the food. If my father was late, we all went to the streetcar station in Ibrahimieh to wait for him. Sometimes we were too tired and went to sleep without any food.

When I was about five or six, my father took me with him to work. Dad, Abdul Meguid, and I were all quite tired as we walked toward our last stop of the day. Before we entered the building, Dad stopped and told me: "You know, you have to be nice to this doctor we are going to visit now. We haven't sold anything today, and we have to bring some food home." When we arrived at the entrance, Dad added, "Smile at him and greet him, you understand?" I nodded. It was past office hours; the doctor sat behind his desk. He must have met my father previously, because he showed no surprise at seeing him with his suitcases. He did notice me, however, and asked my name. To my father's great satisfaction, I answered him in Greek and in a respectful manner.

After looking at some fabrics, the doctor selected two pieces and decided to buy one. When the doctor reached for his wallet to pay, my father pushed me forward and told me in Greek, "Kiss his hand." My pride wounded, I was nearly in tears. I took the doctor's hand and raised my head to look at him, but I could not kiss his hand. Dad was angry. He grabbed me by my shoulder. The doctor stopped him and asked, "Where is that other fabric you were showing me in the beginning? I want to buy it, too."

That night we enjoyed a festive dinner at home. Dad and Mom smiled at us as we devoured the food. They did not eat until we were completely satisfied. Dad sipped his wine and smiled broadly. He poured a few drops of wine into our water glasses, which gave them a nice pink color. "A little red wine is good for your health and will help you sleep," he said, and we all joined in, raising our glasses and cheering, *L'chaim; Stin iyassas* ("To life; to your health" in Hebrew and Greek).

My mother would rub my dad's back at night, and he would tell her in Greek that he had had a tough day "fighting the lions." When I was four or five, I believed that he actually fought real lions, so I developed a deep fascination with them. Mom used to read me stories from an illustrated children's Bible, and I repeatedly asked her to read the story of Samson killing the lion. To me Dad personified Samson. I could visualize him spreading the lion's jaws wide open with his strong bare hands.

One evening I heard Dad telling Mom about an Englishman who had been about to buy a piece of fabric but changed his mind when he found out that my father was Jewish. The man turned his back to my father and declared, "I never buy from Jews. I don't trust them." My father still fumed as he related the story to Mom. He said that he almost punched the Englishman, but Abdul Meguid had pulled my father away. I imagined my father's powerful fist landing on the Englishman's nose and blood pouring from his face.

* * *

Dad was not the only superstitious Greek in Alexandria; all the Greek families we knew in Egypt were superstitious. Most wore a blue stone adorned with a carved or painted eye or a metal amulet in the shape of a five-finger open-handed palm. This object, called a *khamsa* (literally "five" in Arabic), was supposed to protect those who wore it by keeping the evil eye away. Even so, most superstitious Greeks would not walk under a ladder, and if we sneezed, we had to pull one of our ears many times. Even today my cousin Denisica insists that whoever sneezes must pull an ear as a precaution.

To reinforce our immunity against the evil eye, Dad would sneak garlic cloves under our mattresses or place a small garlic clove in our pockets. When we talked about a funeral, a death, or a very ill person, my father would immediately say, *Efghame psariah* ("We ate fish"). Dad believed that fish had the unique ability to prevent any disasters from befalling us.

Several priests lived in our neighborhood because it happened to be the location of a Greek Orthodox church. Many residents considered these priests bad omens because they provided absolution to the dying and the extremely ill. People often tried to avoid the priests by crossing to the other side of the street. Dad took this superstition to an extreme. He could not notice a priest coming his way without rushing after him. When he judged the distance just right, he would spit, and his spittle inevitably landed at the bottom of the priest's black cassock. I witnessed this embarrassing assault many times. My father could hurl his spit from as far as twelve feet away. His accuracy was unerring, and no one ever caught him.

My parents remained faithful to Judaism. Although they celebrated all the holidays and traditions, they did not follow strict Jewish kosher dietary rules. Dad prayed every morning before going to work, but in his own peculiar and unique way. He stood in the doorway to his bedroom, close to the mezuzah. He would look up at a large portrait of his mother that had been painted in Izmir; it showed her with a scarf on her head, a clover behind her ear, and her index finger pointing to her forehead as if to say, "Remember me." My father remembered her every day by kissing her picture and asked for her blessing repeatedly.

Dad would describe his most recent problems and ask for God's forgiveness and help. To pray, he used a velvety white bag that contained his tallith and tefillin, which he held tightly against his heart. He recited the first part of the morning Hebrew prayer from memory. He would then follow up with his own original prayer in Greek—a mixture of formal Hebrew passages and improvised entreaties to reflect the day's particular issues and needs. If any of us was sick, he would passionately plead for our prompt recovery. He repeatedly blessed us one by one. We knew who was in his good graces and who was not by the number of times he pronounced each of our names.

During his morning prayers, especially when we had financial problems, Dad often would curse Mom's family, and she would rush away to cry in another room. When she returned, she had dried her tears, but her eyes remained red. This happened far too many times. My father behaved as tough Cretans did. Often, at the peak of his anger, he would end an argument by telling Mom that only one irreplaceable woman existed in a man's life—his mother.

In reality my father was a good man. Under his rough and explosive exterior, he loved his wife and children, and he sacrificed his health to sustain us in the best way he knew how. Our poverty made him angry and humiliated him, and anyone who gave him the slightest provocation became a target for his frustrations.

Hoping and believing that fate would intervene and help him, my father gambled away a large portion of the little money he made. Every Sunday he visited a Greek coffee shop near our house, where he placed horse-racing bets with a greedy Greek bookmaker. Despite his many losses, my father held an unshakable belief that his next bet would pay off. When we needed to buy something, he would say, "I'll buy it when I win this weekend. Pray for me, and it will happen." In the beginning I prayed fervently, but I soon found out that prayers did not help in such cases.

My father's gambling inspired my brother Léon to invent a way to collect extra pocket money. He would head for the coffee shop where Dad placed his bets. Léon would find just the right moment, as Dad simultaneously reviewed the horses' names on the board and struggled to read the racing book in his hands. Then Léon would pull Dad's coat to grab his attention. Without taking his eyes off his book and the board, Dad would dig into his pocket with his free hand and give Léon whatever coins he found. "Go!" he would say. "This is not a place for you." My brother used to claim that he got his best weekly allowances this way.

Léon was a survivor. He always found ways to make a buck and tried to make the best of any circumstance. He attended the Aghion School, which was sponsored by the Alexandria Jewish community for poor Jewish children whose parents could not afford to send them to French, English, or American schools. When Léon was six or seven, Madame Shakée, his teacher, kept him after class for hitting a boy. She told Léon he had to remain still for an hour. My brother, eager to play with the other boys in the courtyard, begged her to let him go—assuring her that he would never, ever hit a boy again. She ignored him and kept reading her book. In desperation he dug into his pocket and retrieved the only coin he had, one piastre—worth around ten cents. He placed it on her desk and declared: "Here, take it—now let me go!" When Mom came to pick him up, Madame Shakée told her, "Madame Sardas, your son wanted to buy me with one piastre. I've been teaching here for more than thirty years, and this is the first time that someone has tried to bribe me!" She tried to keep a straight face in front of my brother but could not hide her amusement.

* * *

On one rare occasion Dad won big on a trifecta. When he approached the bookmaker to collect his winnings, the bookmaker said he needed a few days to gather the large sum of money. Dad did not mind and returned the following weekend. The bookmaker said he needed a few more days—and continued to postpone the payment week after week. Dad realized that the bookmaker did not plan to pay him, so one Sunday my father and eight strong fellow Cretans showed up at the coffee shop. My father approached the bookmaker at his table and asked him to step outside. The bookmaker answered that he was busy and could not leave the table. My father's friends grabbed him by his shoulders, lifted him, and carried him outside, close to a parked car.

The men asked, "This is your car, right?" The bookmaker nodded. Dad and his friends placed their hands under the car and lifted it high off the ground. Dad then screamed at the bookmaker, "Listen, you bastard, if you do not bring my money by next weekend, we will grab your car." My father got his money the following week.

Our father also liked to have fun, tell jokes, sing, drink, and party. His Cretan friends and relatives invited us over just so he would participate in their celebrations. My father always brought his bouzouki. After eating and drinking, he would play and sing nostalgic songs from their native land. The group circled around him, and the women danced the *kalamatiano*, a Greek line dance. The men sometimes joined them to energize the group, but more often the men danced the *zeibekiko*, an individual dance meant to express happiness, love, nostalgia, and sadness. Late at night we walked home along the empty streets of Ibrahimieh. I tried not to fall asleep in Dad's arms so that he would carry me on his strong shoulders. I would hold his head with my hands, and he added excitement by hopping every three or four steps while he sang Greek songs.

My mother, by contrast, was calm, well mannered, and unselfish. I cannot recall her raising her voice except to call us from the window at dusk when we played in the street. She never raised her hand against any of us, and God knows we often deserved it. Her day was unbelievably busy and long. She would wake up before dawn to prepare our breakfast, which consisted of a piece of bread, a small bit of butter when it was available, and a cup of tea. She then woke each of us up—not an easy task. Mom helped us dress, served us breakfast, checked our schoolbags, and took us to school.

When she returned, she cleaned the house, washed and ironed our clothes, and prepared dinner if Dad had left her money for food. In the afternoon she rushed to bring us home from school, helped each of us with our homework, and gave us something to eat. She then welcomed Dad home and listened patiently to him. After putting us to bed, Mom stayed up sewing for many hours. This was her exhausting daily routine.

Our home lacked space and comfort. She washed our laundry in a small area close to the kitchen that had a drain in the floor—the same place we bathed. She sat on a small stool with a large basin in front of her, rubbed the clothes with her hands, and stopped only to pick up the bar of soap or wipe perspiration from her face. She heated the water in a tin receptacle atop a kerosene Primus stove.

I remember seeing her sewing late at night when I awoke to go to the bathroom. She would put her index finger to her lips to keep me quiet. Under the dim light she patched our clothes. They were passed down from Léon to Saby and then to me. I do not believe that as a child I ever had new clothes. The only new suit I recall wearing was a sailor's uniform, all white with a blue collar. I must have received it at Léon's bar mitzvah; I would have been six. In one of our rare early pictures, the four of us appear well dressed. Only Léon wore a suit with long pants, because long trousers were allowed only after a boy had his bar mitzvah.

Our mother was the most educated of all our relatives and friends. She had mastered written and spoken French, English, Spanish, Turkish, and Ladino. She also learned to speak Greek and Arabic. Whenever our relatives needed to write or read a document in French, Spanish, or English, they asked for her help. She earned their respect not only because of her skills but also because she spared no effort to assist them.

Dad was not the kind of man to take precautions against pregnancy, so my mother was frequently pregnant. She had several miscarriages and abortions before I was born, and at least one after. Given our family's precarious financial situation, I suspect that my arrival was not a particularly happy event.

I cannot recall ever seeing my mother standing idle or taking the time to read a book or a magazine. I do not think she went to a theater or a cinema more than twice after she married. Once, when I was five or six years old, my mother, my father, and I did go see *Romeo and Juliet* with Norma Shearer and Leslie Howard. From her Shakespearean studies, my mother knew several lines by heart. She wiped her tears with her handkerchief. As we left the theater, she held my hand and told me that I looked like Leslie Howard. I left the theater somewhat upset because of the sad ending. I wanted a happy ending so my mother did not have to cry so much.

The only other time I remember my mother going to a theater was the night she accepted our neighbors' invitation to accompany them to a play at the Greek theater near our house. They had only one ticket available, so we all had to stay home with Dad. How surprised he was to see us jumping and laughing when he was expecting us to whine and cry. We crowded into our mom's bedroom and admired her while she applied her makeup. She was beautiful. We kissed her as she headed out the door.

Mom's close friend was Madame Schultz, a French widow with a son, Gerard; they had once been our neighbors. She directed the sewing workshop at Aghion School. Many poor young women worked for her. My two brothers, my sister, and I all attended Aghion. When Denise was nine, however, Mom persuaded the English school to accept her under a special financial arrangement. She wanted Denise to learn English, because it was considered a sophisticated language.

Madame Schultz and Mom shared the same interests, and they enjoyed spending time talking with each other in French. They used to meet on the same day each week to chat while they were shopping at the market in Camp de César, a thirty-minute walk from our house. Mom often took me with her, since she had no one to babysit. During one of their long conversations, I grew impatient and pressed Mom to go home. My mother looked at Madame Schultz helplessly and, pointing at me, signaled that she had no choice but to leave. Madame Schultz disagreed. How could a five-year-old force them to end their conversation? She snatched me away from my mother, held me with one hand, and spanked me several times with the other. "Now," Madame Schultz told my mother, "he's going to be quiet, and we're going to talk." I was shocked. How dare a stranger hit me when my mother had never done so? I freed myself from her grip and kicked her right on her shinbone. She bent over, screaming, "Tyrant! Gangster!" I had heard these names before from my aunt Pauline and my father, and I would hear them many times after that. My mother, upset and apologetic, immediately took me home.

Although Mom lived a hard life, she usually managed to hide from us just how hard it was. When she could not hold back her tears, she would escape to an isolated place to cry.

One day, however, when I was alone with her at home, she could not hide her tears. That day a truck stopped by our house, and a group of men knocked on our door. My parents had fallen behind on the rent. The men had come to inventory and appraise all our furniture. If we did not pay by a certain deadline, they would seize our furniture and evict us. While the men moved from room to room, my mother, one hand over her mouth, could not hold back her tears. I moved close to her. She hugged me and kept saying, "Don't worry, it will be all right." I felt despair at seeing her distraught and tried to kick the man closest to me, but she stopped me.

Eventually Dad found a way to pay the rent before the deadline. We kept our furniture and our home. I do not know how he found the money; he must have borrowed it from Uncle Vita. Dad often borrowed money from Uncle Vita when Aunt Pauline was not present, and my father seldom paid it back.

We occupied the lower level of a two-story house. We gained access to our home through a lobby close to the street. We had only two bedrooms, one for Mom and Dad, the other for the four of us. Léon and Saby shared one bed, Denise and I the other. We had a small kitchen, a toilet, and the small area for bathing and laundry. Its faucet was just a foot above the floor. Ceramic tile covered the floor of our entire house, except for the bedrooms, which had wood floors.

One day when I was five years old and alone with my mother at home, I grew bored. As she rushed with her broom from one room to another, I ran after her, grabbing her by her skirt and saying, "Mom, Mom." Several times she stopped to ask what I wanted, but I did not answer. Finally

I grabbed her legs while she was walking into the kitchen to check the food in the oven. I hung on to her legs and whined: "Ma, Ma." She replied, "Yes, Jacob? I asked you several times what is going on, and you did not answer—tell me what you want."

"I'm hungry!"

"And what is this?" she asked, pointing to the sandwich I held in my hand.

I had no answer. I glanced at my sandwich and felt embarrassed and guilty. I left the kitchen, stormed into the backyard, and threw my sandwich in the garbage. I really just wanted her attention and more of her time—neither of which she could afford to give me that day.

* * *

I was a very active boy when I was little. I did not talk much, but I was always curious and observed what was going on in my surroundings. My behavior was probably influenced by the nickname my father labeled me with soon after I was born. He pointed to the birthmark on my right wrist and the rebel red tuft of hair sticking out from the blond curls on my head and exclaimed in Greek, *Prossexete: aftos ine simathemenos* ("Beware: this one is marked"). Thereafter I was known as O Simathemenos ("the marked one").

According to the gossipy neighborhood Greeks, I got the birthmark because my mother craved fruit during her pregnancy: some people thought it looked like a small ripe banana. The older matrons blamed the birthmark on my father's failure to provide my mother with this fruit during her pregnancy.

With its dark brown color and black dots, the birthmark was noticeable but not particularly conspicuous. One had to be aware of it to see it. My father, however, called attention to it by repeatedly shouting my moniker all over the neighborhood. He called me O Simathemenos at home and in the streets, and from then on, my family and friends used the name, too, whenever I did something especially bad or especially good. They did not miss an opportunity to tease me and make fun of me, which infuriated me and made me feel insecure and helpless. Their harassment was torturing me, and there was no way to stop it. I really thought I was marked by some kind of illness or curse. This went on until one day my mother created an amazing metamorphosis within me. That day, nothing kept her from giving me all her attention, her caring, her love. That day changed my life.

I was around six, and after playing in our street, I rushed home, crying and bleeding from badly scraped knees. My mother asked what happened. I explained that I had fallen while chasing the boys who were teasing me about my birthmark and calling me O Simathemenos! Mom smiled and stood me in front of her. I found comfort inhaling her sweet lavender scent as she wrapped her arms around my shoulders. "Jacob, my son," she said. "You got the mark because you're exceptional—because you're smart. It is a good sign that God gave you. You must be happy that God has chosen you among all the other boys to be the marked one." Encouraged by my wide smile, she continued: "You know, from now on, don't get mad when they tease you—just tell them the mark means you're special."

So I followed my mother's advice, and it worked. My friends' teasing turned to curiosity when I said my mark was a special sign with mystical powers. I grew to enjoy showing it off. I said that every time I needed help, I just rubbed it and would get what I asked for. To convince them, I added, "That is why I'm getting such good grades at school." By repeating my story often, I convinced not only my friends but also myself. Actually, I began to rub my wrist every time I faced a challenge, and the habit stayed with me. Although my birthmark has since faded away, the gesture reminds me that my mother helped me gain confidence and get the better of my anger when people called me O Simathemenos, the marked one.

* * *

We lived on Memphis Street in Ibrahimieh for around six years, from the time I was four until I was ten. Memphis Street was a safe place to play, even late at night. There was practically no traffic; cars were quite a rare sight. We had a roller-skating rink across the street from our house, and the Ibrahimieh Sporting Club was around a hundred yards away. We went into these places to play without being questioned or bothered by anyone. Most of all I liked to watch the basketball games at the club.

The Corcous, a family of four, lived next door to us—the father, Dimitri; the mother, Ralou; a son, Dionysos (nicknamed Nyonyo), who was Léon's age; and a daughter, Katie, or Béba, who was my age. Their house sat between the Ibrahimieh Sporting Club and our house. A five-foot-high wall separated their garden from our alley. The family spoke only Greek, and we communicated with them over that wall. Dimitri Corcou worked as a clerk at Grands Magasins Hannaux, a large department store. He loved to take naps—he took naps on the weekends and sometimes during the week. An almost religious atmosphere surrounded the Corcous' house every time he napped. Everyone respected his resting hours.

What a contrast between our homes! Our house was noisy all the time, even on the rare occasions when Dad rested. Although our house was not dirty, it did not approach the hospital-like cleanliness and austerity of the Corcous'. The major difference was one we children enjoyed: the aroma emanating from Ralou Corcou's kitchen. She was an excellent cook and prepared food all day long. Sometimes she baked cakes and prepared delicious fruit jams. The inviting smells attracted us, and when we were lucky, depending on the time of day and Mrs. Corcou's mood, she would allow us a taste of whatever food she had just prepared.

Mr. Corcou was tall and had white hair and a big mustache. His wife was around four feet six, not even as tall as her husband's chest. Both children also were extremely short. I liked Béba very much. We got along well and liked to play together during our frequent visits to each other's homes, but I did not like Nyonyo, an arrogant and unfriendly boy.

Mr. Corcou and Nyonyo enjoyed hunting with their relatives two or three times a year. After a couple of days they would return in a relative's car loaded with quail, always making certain that we and other neighbors noticed their arrival.

During the several evenings that followed, Mr. Corcou would cook the birds on his back-garden grill. The overwhelming aroma pervaded our home, and we could barely contain our desire to taste a piece of grilled quail. I climbed the wall several times to watch him. He cleaned the quail and marinated them with oregano, red wine, and a mixture of condiments. He patiently stood in front of the grill, turning the quail one by one, and brushing them with his sauce until they were done. He never once offered me even a tiny piece of meat.

One day I noticed a large quail darting through our garden. I hid behind a tree, waited until it came closer, jumped, and caught it. I was exuberant. I kept it in a shoe box with a few holes so the quail could breathe.

That same evening, while Mr. Corcou was cooking on his grill, I climbed atop the wall and showed him my quail. "That is a big fat quail. Do you want me to cook it for you?" he asked.

"Yes," I said. "Can I join you?"

He took the quail and helped me climb over the wall. He held the quail by its legs and quickly slammed its head against a tree. "This way," he explained, "we'll keep the blood in its body; it will give it a better taste."

Then he cleaned it, seasoned it, and placed it on the grill among his own quail. I vigilantly watched to make certain he did not mix mine with his. When it was ready, he placed it on a plate and handed it to me. I ate it instantly. It was delicious. I have since had the opportunity to eat quail in various places; however, none has ever even come close to the taste of the quail I caught in my yard on Memphis Street.

One Sunday afternoon, Léon and Nyonyo got into a fistfight. Nyonyo made a derogatory comment about Jews, and my much taller and stronger brother hit him in the face. Nyonyo ran with his bloody nose into his house and returned with his angry father. Both were holding hunting rifles. Léon dashed into our house and hurriedly explained the conflict to Dad. Mr. Corcou stood against the wall with his gun pointed directly at our door. Nyonyo climbed on top of the wall with his gun in his hand. Mr. Corcou cursed our family furiously. He angrily repeated, *Evrayi! Evrayi!* ("Hebrews! Hebrews!")

My father ordered us to stay in the house. He opened the door and moved toward the Corcous. The door, left ajar, allowed us to watch and listen. The Corcous continued to curse and pointed their guns at my father. My father was wearing a sleeveless undershirt that accentuated his strong arms. They threatened him as he advanced toward them. To our surprise Dad, who usually yelled at the slightest provocation, spoke in a soft, self-contained voice. Pointing to his chest, he said: "You want to shoot? Go ahead—shoot! No one should be allowed to insult anyone's religion; my son did what he had to do because your son insulted the Jews."

Shocked, the Corcous remained quiet, with their guns still aimed at him.

Dad moved even closer to them and continued: "You two don't scare me with your guns. I've faced death many times. As a Jew, I fought for Greece and got this as a result of a face-to-face with Turkish soldiers." He lifted his pants and showed them a large scar on his thigh. He asked them, "And what have you done for Greece?" When Dad sensed they were impressed, he raised his voice and said, "If you really want to fight, come out in the street, and fight like men!"

They offered no answer and remained positioned with their guns when Dad left and entered our house. We stared at the Corcous. They didn't know what to do; they waited a few more moments and then went back inside their house.

Dad told Léon, "They won't bother you anymore." Jubilant, we all jumped onto my father, hung onto his arms, and laughed joyfully. We were proud of him.

We did not speak to the Corcous for many weeks. Béba stopped visiting our house, and we stopped going to theirs. I missed her and the long chats and play sessions we enjoyed in our garden. I do not know how the families reconciled. I believe my mother took the first step when she greeted Mrs. Corcou as they met on the street. Then we had a party. The Corcous brought some of their fine food, and we brought some of ours. We lined up the plates and glasses on top of the wall. I remember my father rushed into our house to grab a flask of red wine and his bouzouki. We toasted, sang, and danced. We never had another fight. Dad was right. Nyonyo never bothered us again.

Béba and I continued to spend many hours in the garden playing and talking. We would lie down on the grass, stare at the sky, and talk about whatever entered our minds. She enjoyed teaching me Greek. Although we spoke fluent Greek at home, we never learned to read and write it because we did not attend a Greek school. Our school, Aghion, offered French and Hebrew to students in the lower grades and Arabic to students in the higher grades.

Béba brought her schoolbooks over, read me stories, and occasionally let me hold the books so I could see the illustrations. She loved playing teacher, and I enjoyed it. With her help I learned Greek children's songs, the Greek national anthem, and how to read and write a bit of Greek.

* * *

My brother Saby was a sickly child who suffered from chronic strep throat and nephritis. His throat infections affected his kidneys, and that often caused him to wet his bed. That meant my mother had to wash the sheets frequently. Because of his frail health Saby remained our father's pet. When we wanted Dad to say yes to something, we always pushed Saby to ask for it.

Saby also was the only one who could stay home from school without having to endure lengthy interrogations. The rest of us could stay home only after our parents determined we had a high fever and were not faking. To make sure, Dad would stick a tongue depressor in our mouths and look deep in our throats for any trace of infection. The exam was thorough and painful. When we succeeded in skipping school without being sick, we called it "making *shampa*"; among us, Saby was the *shampa* specialist. If we were sick and did stay home, we had to endure a purge of castor oil or sodium sulfate; both tasted awful. If we coughed or had a cold, Dad used ventouses (suction cups) on our backs; they hurt and left dark round marks wherever he had applied them. According to him, the darker the spots, the better. It meant that the ventouses had sucked the cold and bad germs out of our bodies.

But Dad's favorite cure for everything was a purging. Strep throats, indigestion, flu, toothaches, headaches—any indisposition required the same treatment: we had to stay in bed and take the purge. As for himself, my father never waited for sickness to take his purge. He went to the beach on Sundays and held a bottle of sodium sulfate and half a lemon in one hand. With his free arm, he swam on his side away from the shore and other bathers. When he had swum far enough, he added clean seawater to the mixture in the bottle, drank it, and sucked the half lemon. What we considered a painful ordeal represented an enjoyable ritual to our father. He would say, "It's time to take the purge."

Despite our precarious financial situation and the worries our parents endured, my siblings and I managed to have more joyful moments than sad ones. Mom always found a way to provide us with inexpensive toys and games. She taught us to play *bataille navale*, a battleship game. For this we used a paper on which we drew two large squares—one for our ships and the other to mark our calls. We played checkers with white and black beans on a checkered tablecloth, and she even made a large ball from our old worn-out socks, which we used when we played soccer in the street outside our house. During spring and summer she would not miss an opportunity to take us to the beach. She used to say, "We have the best entertainment of all here, close to home. The Mediterranean Sea has the most beautiful beaches in the world, and they cost us nothing."

She always tried to make our homework interesting and fun. She would tell us a short story or an anecdote related to our homework to fix it in our minds. When I read about the parting of the Red Sea by Moses, she opened an atlas and showed me the Red Sea's location. She then showed me the English Channel, which the French call La Manche. However, *manche* also means "sleeve" in French. One day, as she closed the atlas, I knew by the look on her face that she was ready to tell me a story. "When I was a little girl, I attended a French school, and in my class we had to recite passages from the Passover Haggadah about the Jewish exodus from Egypt." One at a time, the students would go up to the front of the room and recite, in French, various passages for the teacher, who then asked questions about the recitation. The teacher asked one girl to name the famous sea involved. The student did not know the answer. Seeking help, she glanced at a friend seated in the front row, who wore a bright red dress with long sleeves. Her friend held up one of her red sleeves, thinking the reciting student would guess that the answer was the Red Sea. The student answered in a loud and confident voice, "La Manche" ("the English Channel"). She realized her mistake only when the class exploded with laughter.

I did not know if the story was true, but certainly my mother entertained me. And I never forgot that it was the Red Sea the Jews crossed. Her story also taught me that cheating does not pay.

She also wanted us to always stick together and remain supportive of one another. She once demonstrated the importance of solidarity with a few wooden sticks that she lined up on the table. "See," she said, "how easy it is to break these four sticks one by one?" Then, taking four sticks together, she continued, "And how difficult, if not impossible, it is to break them when they are unified?" Her influence inspired the four of us to remain united and close during all these years. We have had many fights among us, but we always reconcile as if nothing has happened. Even today we spare no effort to help each other.

In Ibrahimieh, when we were kids, other children often would try to pick on one of us. We always ran to each other's rescue. One day, Saby and an Arab boy, who was much bigger than he was, were yelling at each other in front of our house. Saby threatened his opponent by pointing to his own biceps, trying to scare him. As Saby showed off his biceps and repeated, *Shooftey dah?* ("Have you seen this?"), the Arab boy kneeled down, placed his head between my brother's legs, lifted him in the air, and slammed him to the ground. With an astonished look on his face, Saby sprawled on the pavement, his fingers still touching his biceps. That was pretty funny.

Léon and I ran toward him, ready to help, but Saby stood and held his hand up: he wanted us to wait. He wanted a fair fight with his opponent. In a matter of seconds my brother won with a grip that never failed him at wrestling. He would wait for the right moment, then put his right arm around his opponent's neck and squeeze it with both arms until his adversary fell to the floor, gasping for air. Saby called the grip *el kamasha*—"the pincers"—and it proved infallible.

Even though I was younger, I always insisted on participating in games with my brothers. Léon was seven years older and Saby four years older, but this age difference did not bother me. After a while I think it no longer bothered them. One morning Mom had something important to do, probably a visit to a doctor. Since I was only five and could not stay home alone, she asked Denise to take me with her to school in the morning and then, at lunchtime, to Madame Schultz's sewing shop, where my sister ate her lunch and hung out with the young women who worked there.

At school Denise's teacher asked me to sit in the last row. She gave me some papers and colored pencils to help me pass the time. That day each student stood in front of the teacher's desk to recite the multiplication tables. I had been listening to my brothers and sister recite multiplication tables for several years, long enough to learn them by heart. They used to sing them to make them easier to remember. As the girls recited multiplication at the teacher's desk, I remained absorbed in my drawings and sang my multiplication tables in a low, soft voice. I was having a good time. One girl next to me yelled excitedly, "Miss! Miss! Jacob knows them! Denise's brother knows all the multiplication tables. I heard him!"

The teacher asked me to come to her desk and recite what I knew. I sang all the tables from one to ten without stopping and without hesitation. The teacher applauded, followed by the whole class. Then she hugged me and said, "You're a smart young boy." She gave me a piece of candy. I felt happy, but I really did not understand the big fuss. For me the multiplication tables were just a song I had learned by hearing it thousands of times. Denise was the happiest and proudest student that day.

* * *

If Saby was my father's pet, Léon was my mother's, her firstborn child of love. He also had dark hair and resembled her side of the family. When he misbehaved, my father called him Beja. Given my father's feelings toward my mother's family, this was not a compliment. When I was six, Léon was already a teenager and had different and more expensive needs than the rest of us. Mom knew quite well that she would have to provide the kind of support that my brother needed at that age.

Whenever she could save some money, she secretly gave it to Léon. This allowed him to go to the movies and hang out with his friends on the weekends, a luxury the rest of us could not afford. She spent more time working with him on his studies and homework. She also made sure that his clothes were clean and nice, because she knew that clothes were important to teenagers.

Léon was a smart, devilish kid who always found a way to profit from a situation. He found ways to take our toys, money, and food. As I grew up, Léon claimed that I owed my good school grades to him. He recalled that when I was a toddler he often took me out in the stroller and used it as a scooter. He would climb on the back, roll away at full speed, and then jump off when he lost control. The stroller usually crashed against a wall or a tree and ended upside down with me in it. "You hit your head so many times that it shook your brains and turned you into a smarter boy!"

Dad was aware of Léon's misbehavior. Whenever one of us cried or screamed, Dad ran directly to Léon and hit him. Usually Dad was right—Léon was guilty—except once when Saby whined and cried while he was in another room with Léon. Dad rushed in as usual and hit Léon with a heavy hand. Afterward Léon confronted Saby and demanded he tell Dad why he had been crying. Saby, still whining, explained that he had a stomachache. My father never missed a beat. He looked at Léon and said, "That's fine. Next time you really deserve it, remind me not to hit you, and we'll be even."

When I was six or seven, Mom told Léon that, at fourteen, he could be in charge of escorting us to and from school, thus saving her the time she took to perform that task each day. So every morning Dad gave him the money we all needed to take the streetcar to school and back. A few weeks later Léon asked if we wanted to eat peanuts and melon seeds, play with a ball, and walk home from school instead of taking the streetcar. He did not wait for our approval. "It will be more fun; you'll see." Each day he urged us to walk more briskly. He bought some peanuts and seeds for a few pennies and gave us one of the balls Mom had sewn together from old socks. We did not complain, and we knew that we could not say a word about this arrangement to our parents because we feared Léon's anger.

This routine continued for a long time. Our parents did not suspect the truth. They noticed only that the soles of our shoes were wearing out faster than usual. One afternoon Dad came home from work earlier than expected, and from his streetcar window he noticed us walking home. He was angry, and he told Mom what he had seen. As soon as we arrived home, she ran to open the door and told Léon that Dad had discovered what was going on and was furious. Léon thereupon locked himself in the water closet, where he often went to hide from my father's ire. He stayed there a long time, until Mom calmed Dad down. My father yelled through the door, "Léon, you are one more Beja who is ruining me with all the money I spend repairing your shoes."

* * *

One weekend, Denise, then twelve, and our cousin Denisica, then ten, were eager to go downtown. They wanted to look in the beautiful store windows and eat pastries. Both had managed to save enough money to spend a special Saturday afternoon doing just that. They even chose in advance the pastry they would eat and talked about it during the week.

But at their age girls were not allowed out on their own in downtown Alexandria, yet neither wanted to spend the day under the watchful eye of their parents. Léon was their only hope. Using their best manners, they begged him to chaperone them downtown for a few hours. After refusing for a long time, he finally accepted on one condition—he would hold their money, because it would not be appropriate for the girls to pay when there was an older boy accompanying them. They negotiated. "We consent, but you have to let us buy pastries at the Grand Trianon or Athineos."

"Yes, of course," he agreed.

First they window-shopped. When they asked to visit the Trianon, he took them there; they stared at the pastries and cakes in its window. When they tried to enter, Léon stopped them. He assured them that Athineos offered a better choice. When they arrived at Athineos, they stared at the appetizing displays in its windows and started to enter the store. He stopped them and, looking at his watch, declared, "I have an appointment with my friends, so we have to go home right now." When they protested, he replied, "Well, you have seen all you wanted through the windows. If you want me to take you out next time, stop complaining and don't you dare report anything about this to our parents." He took them home and kept their money. Denise and Denisica told no one about his trickery because they wanted to make more trips downtown.

With the money Mom gave him, Léon had bought a beautiful dark green Bakelite pocket flashlight with black stripes. It was the size of his palm. We all wanted to hold it and play with it, but Léon would not allow us to touch it. He never let it out of his sight; he even slept with it.

One summer afternoon we all gathered at the wall beneath the Corcous' window. That wall, which separated their garden from the street, was taller than the wall between their garden and our alley. My mother was standing in the street and talking with Ralou Corcou, who looked out her window. Mom had helped me climb up and sit on the wall with my legs hanging down. I faced the street, where Mom, Béba, Denise, and my two brothers stood. My back was to the Corcous' garden. I do not know why, but suddenly Léon lifted my legs and pushed me over the wall. I fell straight down like an arrow, headfirst, into the Corcous' garden. My head landed only a couple of inches from the sharp garden tools that were kept there. I could have been killed. Everyone screamed, fearing the worst.

Mrs. Corcou and my mother carried me to my bed, and, as I was feeling chills, they covered me with heavy blankets. I was dizzy and nauseated as I shivered under the blankets. Mom gave me a bottle of Spathis lemonade, which Mrs. Corcou had brought from her house. Mom heated it, and I sipped while lying in bed. The drink warmed me, and although I still felt sick, somehow I did not mind. I had the undivided attention of my mother and all the people around my bed. Above all, I was drinking a Spathis, an expensive lemonade we got only on special occasions.

After I rested for a while, Léon, remorseful and deeply concerned about Dad's furious reaction, came to me, put his arm around me, and handed me his prized flashlight. He said, "Take it; it's yours." I could not believe it. The beautiful dark green flashlight was mine. My brother was not so selfish after all.

I must have fallen asleep for a long time, because when I opened my eyes the room was dark. Léon was sitting by my side, trying to take back the flashlight, which was still firmly grasped in my hand. When he noticed that I had awakened, he asked me to give it back to him. I responded, "But you offered it to me!" He paused, then said he wanted to make sure the batteries were in good shape. He took the flashlight, examined it, and said, "I'm taking it back because now you're doing better." He then left the room with the flashlight in his hand.

One Saturday afternoon we watched Léon dash through our front door and head straight for the water closet, locking the door behind him. He was wearing a swimsuit, had no shoes on, and his whole body was covered with sweat. Mom ran anxiously after him and spoke to him through the door. At her insistence he finally came out and told her what had happened. He had been playing with friends at the beach, where one of his friends had a cabana in which they changed clothes. A group of other boys challenged Léon and his buddies to a beach soccer game. Léon's team won and celebrated their victory with cheers. The leader of the opposing team then drew a Star of David on the wet sand and spat on it, saying, "Here's for you, you bunch of dirty Jews." He had his feet in the water, and my brother lifted a large stone and threw it on the boy's foot. The stone landed on the boy's big toe and pulled the nail off. The shallow seawater grew red with blood, and the boy screamed. My brother ran home and left all his belongings in the cabana. While the boy continued to scream, the rest of his team chased after my brother. As he told the story, Léon calmed down. "I ran a lot faster than they did," he declared.

Mom could not ask him to go back and recover his belongings. She asked for the exact location of the cabana where Léon had left his clothes. She waited another hour, went to the beach, and came back with my brother's belongings. We could not afford to lose them.

* * *

My brothers were opposites. Léon, outgoing and devilish, always tried to have fun and seek adventures. He was disorganized and often in trouble. Saby, poised and thoughtful, was quiet and well organized. Saby was also a bit of a dreamer. Late one afternoon, while sitting on the couch, he concentrated on memorizing a Hebrew lesson about Noah and the flood. The section started with *Noah Hatzaddik* ("Noah the faithful"). Saby pronounced these first words in a cheerful, loud voice, but soon his eyes closed; he was half asleep. After a minute or so he would suddenly lift his head and start over again, repeating *Noah Hatzaddik*. He would then close his eyes. This continued a few more times until Mom finally asked him to go to bed and study his lesson early the next morning. Even now we jokingly refer to Saby as Noah Hatzaddik. He is the first one to laugh about it.

Neither Léon nor Saby changed when they grew up. As a young adult, Léon remained an extrovert and opportunist. He took life lightly and collected jokes to make his audience laugh. He was popular with the girls because he had a nice voice similar to that of Tino Rossi, the French singer and movie star who was popular back then. At the same time, Saby was quiet, thrifty, disciplined, and thoughtful. He always planned his activities. He ignored us and wanted us to ignore what he was up to. Saby also worried about the future. Seeking to improve his position and find one with security, he changed jobs frequently. He always asked his interviewer, *Est-ce qu'il y a de l'avenir?* ("Does it have a good future?")

* * *

Aunt Pauline, and especially Uncle Vita, spoiled Denisica, their only child. She ended up getting practically anything she wanted. If she could not persuade her mother to buy something for her, she knew that her father would indulge her. She liked to spend most weekends at our house. She played with Denise, and whenever I could not play with my brothers, I called Béba, my friend from next door, and we joined Denise and Denisica in their games.

Denise was the nicest among us. She never had a fight with any of us. She was the most obedient child in the family. We respected and protected her. After all, she was the only girl among three strong brothers. She had beautiful hazel eyes and curly blond hair. My mother liked to style Denise's hair in the manner of Shirley Temple's.

Denise served as the second woman in command of our home. Our mother taught her how to cook and sew at an early age, and they had a close relationship. Whenever my mother went on an errand, she asked my sister to take care of the food and finish some household chores. Before leaving, our mother used to slip her apron around my sister's neck as a symbol of the authority and responsibility Mom was bestowing on her. My sister felt quite proud; she loved wearing her mother's apron.

Although she was two years younger than Denise, Denisica always wanted to copy my sister and outdo her in all respects. She loved Denise, but at the same time she was jealous of her. When Denise attended the English Academy in Alexandria, Denisica wanted to enroll there, too, but she was not old enough to be admitted. Denisica was furious that she could not learn English, as my sister was doing. She asked Denise to lend her one of her English textbooks and promised to return it the next day. When my sister went back to pick it up, she called up to Denisica from the street and asked her to bring it down. Denisica answered from the balcony, "Get in the building, and I'll come downstairs to give it to you." When Denise entered the building, she found pieces of her book scattered all over the stairs. Denisica had cut each page of the book into small pieces, and they covered all four floors, from the ground floor up to the family's apartment.

When Denise turned eleven, Mom bought her a pair of shoes with slightly high heels. "You're becoming a beautiful demoiselle," Mom told her. "These are your first high-heeled shoes. Wear them in good health." Denisica threw a fit. She, too, wanted high heels. Her parents refused to buy high heels for a nine-year-old—it just was not proper. She would have to wait another two years, her parents said.

A few weeks later, when Denise visited her, Denisica asked to try on her shoes. She put them on and started walking. When she came close to the open window, she took one shoe off and threw it out into the street as far as she could. Denise was dumbfounded; she ran outside but could not find the shoe. My mother had to use all her ingenuity to save enough money to buy a new pair.

One day Denisica showed up for a visit but refused to come inside. Instead she kept knocking on the door. When I finally opened it to see what her problem was, she slipped her wrist inside to show off her new watch, a gift from her father. We felt outraged—how could she get a watch at her age?

It just was not fair for a spoiled nine-year-old to come to our house to show off her new watch. I was angry and revolted. I grabbed a metal plate from a nearby table, slammed it against her wrist, and smashed her new watch to pieces. She stared at the little pieces of her watch scattered across the floor, cried, and ran away just as her mother was arriving. Her mother called me all sorts of names: *fonias* ("gangster"); *tirannay* ("tyrant"); Matathias. Matathias, a Cretan relative from Chania, was famous for his strength. Rumors circulated that one night, after he had had many drinks, he stopped a streetcar in Alexandria by standing in front of it, defying the conductor, and holding a group of policemen at bay. I disliked being called a gangster and a tyrant, but I did not mind being called Matathias. He was doing bad things, but he was strong.

I ran out the back door to escape my aunt's anger and the reaction of my parents, who rarely contradicted her. Aunt Pauline was an obese woman with beautiful features, but her weight affected her physically and emotionally. She had difficulty walking and was always short of breath. Because she was sick most of the time, her Cretan friends and relatives worked hard not to upset her. I am sure that she must have been sick when she went home that day. I felt sorry for her—but not for her daughter.

* * *

A movie theater, La Gaîté, was located on Ibrahimieh Street, not far from our house. On Saturday afternoons when I was seven or eight, I often walked to the theater and spent a long time looking at the posters on its walls—I did not have enough money to buy a ticket. By scrutinizing the faces of the actors, I created my own version of the movie. After a couple of hours I returned home satisfied, as if I had actually attended the film.

At that time theaters were showing movies with cliff-hanger endings about heroes such as Zorro, the Lone Ranger, and Captain Marvel. Sometimes my friends would see these movies with their parents and come out of the theater to find me still contemplating the pictures on the walls. They thought that I had just come out of the theater, as they had, and they stopped for a short time to talk about how much they enjoyed the movie. They always asked me if I liked the scenes they described, and of course I agreed with them.

I followed that routine for a long time, but I eventually reached the point where looking at the posters proved unsatisfactory. The short time my friends spent telling me about their favorite parts made me eager to actually go inside and finally watch the movie. One afternoon, in an act of desperation, I sneaked in with some children entering the theater with their parents. I stood in a long line, and the group of us entered so fast that the man who was checking the tickets did not notice me. I did this many times. I became skilled at choosing the right time, the right crowd, and the right way to sneak in.

One Saturday afternoon Denisica followed me to the theater. When she saw me sneak in, she rushed in behind two adults. She was caught when she was only a few steps inside. I heard her voice while I rapidly advanced into the dark theater and took a seat far from the entrance, close to a large family with children. I could hear Denisica's piercing voice as the theater's employee dragged her outside. She screamed, "But my cousin went in also; he's inside!" The employees tried to locate me with a flashlight, but they did not find me.

I did not mind having Denisica participate in some of our games; she was funny and cheerful. I was, however, always on my guard. One evening Mom took the four of us to visit Aunt Pauline. My father and Uncle Vita were still at work. While my mother was busy with Aunt Pauline in a separate room, Denise, Denisica, and I played in Denisica's bedroom.

Mom called us when it was time to leave. I left the room, but when Denise tried to follow me, Denisica held her by her shoulders and would not let Denise go. I did not like what Denisica was doing and came back to free my sister. "Let her go," I demanded. As soon as I said that, Denisica slapped me with all her might and ran to the bathroom and locked herself in. Alerted by the noise and the screaming, my mother, my brothers, and Aunt Pauline rushed into the room. I was fuming and knocking on the bathroom door.

My blood was boiling; my face was red partially from the slap but mostly from my anger. Before even inquiring what had happened, Aunt Pauline pointed at me and screamed, "Look at his face! He wants to kill my daughter! He is a gangster! *Fonias, tirannay*, Matathias! That's why he is the Simathemenos; he was marked by God." Her blame, on top of the slap, fueled my anger. As my aunt continued to taunt me, I could not take it anymore. I needed to run away.

I ran out the front door and down the stairs. Mom told Léon to run after me. She knew I could hurt myself, given my emotional state. I ran like a mad boy in the streets; my brother, only a few yards behind me, could not manage to catch me. We must have run half a mile before we reached the streetcar tracks near Ibrahimieh station. Without looking to see if a streetcar was coming, I continued running. My brother slowed down to let a streetcar pass. This place was usually busy, with streetcars going both ways. Crossing the double tracks was indeed a crazy act of despair. Certain that I would be hit by a speeding streetcar, my brother could only watch helplessly as I crossed to the station at full speed. By pure luck I escaped death that evening. My brother eventually caught me near our house. The run had calmed me down, but I did not forget the incident.

Denisica had not dared return to our house. When she and her parents thought enough time had passed, she showed up at the Corcous' house while Denise and I were there. Before Denisica could get inside, I was all over her. I threw her on the ground and beat her up. I stopped only when my sister and Mrs. Corcou pulled me away. Denisica left crying, and we learned later on that she had a high fever from the beating.

* * *

One afternoon Denise, Denisica, Béba, and I were in the Corcous' kitchen, chatting and having fun. Mrs. Corcou was in the living room with her cousins. She did not want us to stay in the kitchen, but she agreed on the condition that we would not stay long and that we would keep away from the stove. Mrs. Corcou was preparing strawberry jam in a large pot. A strong, delicious aroma of sugar, strawberry, and cinnamon filled the air. We would not leave the kitchen, although Mrs. Corcou asked us to several times. In whispers we agreed not to answer, hoping that she would come to the kitchen and perhaps let us taste that delicious jam. Our plan didn't work. With a firmer voice Mrs. Corcou asked us to leave the kitchen immediately and go play elsewhere. We were disappointed, and everyone but Denisica left the kitchen. She stayed behind, looked around to make certain no one was coming in, approached the stove, and spat in the boiling pot of jam. But Mrs. Corcou's cousin saw her do it in the large mirror on the wall in front of the couch she was sitting on. The cousin could not believe what she had just witnessed. She stood up and screamed, "Ralou, that little girl spat in your jam!" Denisica ran away. Out in the street we asked her why she had done it. She looked at us with her mischievous eyes and replied, "She should have given us a taste of that jam."

At age nine Denisica dressed like a girl twice her age. Whenever she had her picture taken, she would always ask the photographer to wait a few seconds so that she could pose like a diva. Although she was short, she became a gorgeous teenager. At fourteen she attracted young men in their twenties. She began flirting at a young age and married at sixteen.

Our constant fights came to an end in a sudden and unexpected way. One day when I was nine, I was walking on Memphis Street, and two young boys followed me, singing, *Ya yahoudi ya mayas ya harami el libass* ("You braggart, you lying Jew, you robber of underwear"). They started attacking me, and I had a hard time defending myself. Suddenly I noticed Denisica running to my rescue. She jumped on one of my attackers, pulled his hair, scratched his face, and bit him. Working together, we soon had the upper hand; our attackers fled. That day Denisica and I were on excellent terms. We laughed about what happened and played together in our garden for a long time. After she fought like that for me, I considered her an integral part of our family team; she had paid the entry fee. We did not fight anymore. We were growing up. We soon had other distractions and concerns, not the least of which was World War II.

* * *

Our home sat between the Corcous' house and that of "the rich Italians," our neighbors to the west. This family of three, a father, mother, and son about my age, lived in a sumptuous two-story house, behind which was a beautiful, large garden filled with colorful flowers and imposing trees. We could catch glimpses of the family over the short wall that separated our side alley from their garden. We saw them only a few times during all the years we lived in our house. They never talked to us or to any of our neighbors.

One day, while I entertained myself in the alley, the ball I was playing with flew into their garden. As I hoisted myself over the wall, the son appeared and picked up the ball, as if to throw it back to me. When he realized that I was about to jump, he held on to the ball and asked me in broken French if I wanted to play with him. I eagerly assented and jumped into his garden. We played for a while, and then he took me into his orchard. He picked up some oranges and mangoes and handed them to me when I climbed back over to my house; before he left, we decided to meet again. Excited, I carried the fruits home and told my mother I had made a new friend. She taught me a few Italian words to try on him during our next playdate. We met a few times after that and played in his beautiful garden and orchard, but we were never allowed inside his house.

One time his mother, a beautiful dark-haired woman, and her servant, who was carrying a rocking horse in his arms, approached us. She asked if I wanted the horse. She spoke perfect French but with an unfamiliar accent. I thought she was asking me if I wanted to play with it. I looked at my friend to see if he wanted us to play with the horse. She understood my confusion and made it clear that she was offering the horse for me to take home. It was mine if I wanted it.

I could not believe what was happening. How could anyone offer me such an expensive toy? "Come on," she said and pointed to the servant. "He will carry it over to your house." The man followed me home, placed the precious offering on our doorstep, and left. My mother opened the door and was surprised to see the rocking horse. I excitedly explained. "The Italian lady gave it to me," I kept repeating while rubbing my birthmark nervously. I knew Mom was proud and did not like us to accept money or gifts from people outside the family, so I begged her not to force me to return it. She smiled, probably because I was so happy. As a gesture of approval and as a precaution, she took an alcohol-soaked cloth and thoroughly wiped the horse from head to toe.

The horse was beautiful—all white with a black head, black eyes, and a black saddle. It had two red handles on its head, by its ears. With the paint somewhat faded, it looked used, but that did not bother me. I had a horse that my parents could not afford, a horse on which I could sit and imagine all kinds of adventures. I could daydream to my heart's content, inspired by the movies I saw at La Gaîté.

I spent hours and hours riding that horse. I was Zorro, the Lone Ranger, and many other invincible heroes. I spent some of my happiest days rocking on the horse, exploring all kinds of exciting and dangerous territory full of enemies. I saved many people, and in every adventure I freed a beautiful girl just seconds before her certain death.

But I did not have many more opportunities to play with my Italian friend. One day a military truck stopped in front of their house. English and Egyptian soldiers barged right onto their property. We did not find out what happened, but we never saw them again. The house remained vacant as long as we lived on Memphis Street.

* * *

Life went on as usual until Germany attacked Poland in September of 1939. World War II began, and our lives became more eventful. We started to see many more English soldiers as well as soldiers of unfamiliar nationalities. We learned to recognize them by their various military uniforms. On weekends they came in large groups to the roller-skating rink across from our house. They were all very friendly and loved to skate with us. Churchill's reassuring face, with his two fingers signaling *V* for victory, appeared on posters and in newspapers.

Then the city of Alexandria began to impose strict blackout rules. We had to cover all our windows with thick black paper. In some buildings people dug shelters in the basement. Alarm drills prepared us for enemy raids. At night searchlights swept the sky, probing for enemy planes.

One Saturday evening—June 22, 1940—all those drills proved useful when we endured our first air raid (conducted by the Italians, we learned later). A couple of bombs razed a few homes in Ibrahimieh some distance from ours. We all ran out the next morning to inspect the damage. The only shelter in our neighborhood was a few hundred yards from our house. Even so, we did not always go there. We preferred to stay home and either sleep or watch the sky from our windows in an attempt to spot an enemy plane among the flashing lights and antiaircraft fire.

Late one night during a raid, probably later that same summer, Denise entered our completely dark bedroom. She looked through the window and started screaming, "I can see the German plane! And now I can see the bombs falling!" We all laughed and made fun of her. Léon pushed her aside to see what was going on, ready to prove her silly. He opened the window a bit wider and kept imitating Denise: "Yes, I can see them; now they are throwing some banana peels and some oranges—" He was interrupted by a huge explosion that shook our entire house. The window from which my brother had been watching was blown away. Fortunately, it burst outward. Had it imploded, he would have died instantly. He escaped with a superficial scratch on his forehead. We never again watched raids from the windows.

We matured more rapidly during the war. Each of us had clothes packed in case of raids. We had to be prepared to leave the house at any moment. During that time I learned to get dressed on my own, without my mother's supervision, but tying my shoes always slowed me down.

One year before his graduation from high school, in 1940, Léon got a job at Agami, a brokerage house. He was Agami's trader at the Alexandria stock exchange, la Bourse des Valeurs, as it was known in Egypt. Despite his youth Léon rapidly learned the complexity of the trade and proved a valuable asset to Agami. He became a pleasant and popular figure whose outgoing personality and loud voice distinguished him from other traders. His bosses were pleased with his performance, and this experience served him well later on.

As a teenager, Léon made enough money to cover his financial needs. Saby and I continued to attend the Aghion School while Denise went to the English Academy. Meanwhile the war grew fiercer. The Germans and Italians bombed Alexandria more heavily and more frequently. The Italian army, already present in Libya, was preparing to invade North Africa, starting with Alexandria.

* * *

One day our parents told us they had to leave for an important appointment. When they returned, they gathered us around the kitchen table and told us that Mom had to undergo surgery. They said it was not serious but that she had to be hospitalized for a few days. My mother added, "Do not forget what I have always told you: remain united. You need to help each other while I am at the hospital." She stopped herself from crying in front of us, and after a few seconds she said, "God will be watching over you. If you all behave well, do your homework, and take care of yourselves, I will be all right, and God will bring me back to you."

The next morning she packed a small suitcase. Before leaving for the hospital with my father, she took us all in her arms and kissed each one of us many times. She then took Denise aside and put her favorite apron around Denise's neck. "Now, while I'm gone, you are the woman of our family; you are the mother of this house. I'm very proud of you." Tears were pouring down Denise's face and Mom's face. When she talks about the day Mom left to go to the hospital, Denise, who was twelve at the time, still sobs and cannot finish her sentence.

We never behaved as well as we did during Mom's stay at the hospital. Although Dad did what he could to help us, we learned to do several things on our own. We prepared our own breakfast with the help of Denise, who proudly wore Mom's apron. Léon, who was seventeen, helped us with our homework, and Saby, then fourteen, finished his quickly. Even after two weeks we were not allowed to visit her, but we were told that the operation had gone well and that the doctor had removed a large fibroma, a benign fibrous tumor, from her belly. She was feeling better and would be back with us soon.

The day before Mom was to be released from the hospital, a Friday, we all went to visit her there. When we got to her room, Mom was sitting on her bed; she smiled broadly when she saw all of us around her. One by one we gave her a long, warm hug. We were all extremely happy. After a long visit we had to leave and expressed our joyful anticipation that we would see her in the morning. Saby told us later that before we left her room, he turned back to look at Mom and was shocked to see her sobbing and drying her tears with a handkerchief. He could not understand why. Only seconds earlier she had been smiling and cheerful.

* * *

On Saturday, September 7, 1940, a few days before my tenth birthday, we woke up early. We had not slept well the night before, both because we were excited about Mom's return and because a long raid had kept us awake with bombs exploding close to our neighborhood.

Denise woke up before any of us. She prepared our breakfast, hot tea with milk and bread; then she swept the floor, cleaned the furniture, and made sure that everything was neat and in place. As Dad prepared to go to the hospital and bring Mom home, the doorbell rang. My father opened the door and found Madame Schultz standing there. She pulled him outside and whispered a few words in his ear. My father screamed, "No! No! Oh, God, why?" He embraced Madame Schultz. They cried loudly in each other's arms.

We had no phone, so the hospital had called Madame Schultz; our mother had died early that morning. During the raid another patient in Mom's room had needed help. Mom got out of bed to help the patient but fell to the floor after taking a few steps. According to what the Greek patient told Madame Schultz, Mom repeatedly whispered in Greek *Khano ton kosmo* ("I'm losing the world") as she lay on the floor. She died of a pulmonary embolism. The four of us froze as we watched Madame Schultz and Dad sobbing. We could not understand what had happened. Léon finally broke the silence and asked, "Are you sure, Madame Schultz?

Maybe it's a mistake. She may have fainted; maybe she did not die." Madame Schultz took Léon in her arms. "Yes, unfortunately, she is dead, and the funeral will take place tomorrow," she said as tears ran down her cheeks. Denise was still wearing Mom's apron. She took it off and threw it in the garbage can. My sister has never worn an apron since.

My brothers and sister started crying after they absorbed the news. I could not. I wanted to, but tears would not come. Emptiness invaded my body. I remained puzzled and confused; even my magic birthmark couldn't help. A few days earlier our French teacher had asked us to write a description of what we would like to receive as a gift for the upcoming holidays. With the Jewish New Year and my birthday only a few days away, I had rushed to finish my homework. When the teacher returned the papers with her notes, she held on to mine. I got nervous, thinking perhaps I had made too many spelling mistakes. Instead the teacher looked at me and said, "I want to read to all of you the wonderful present that Jacob wants for his birthday." She paused for a few seconds and added, "This is what he wrote: 'My best present will be when my mother comes home from the hospital before my birthday.'"

But after my mother's death I was angry and rebellious. How could God do this to us? We were behaving well the whole time, as Mom had asked us to. We did not fight and did nothing bad. Why did God punish us? I could not understand it, and I could not accept it. Was this God's present for my birthday? What did I do wrong? I realized I was only ten and had lost my mother forever. I would never again see her reassuring smile or hear her sweet voice. That day, while everyone cried and explained to the neighbors what had happened, I opened the door and ran like a lunatic into the surrounding streets of Ibrahimieh. When I came back home, out of breath, I heard the neighbors ask my brothers if I was aware of what had happened. No one could understand what I felt. They thought that I was too young to realize the extent of our loss, yet I fully understood that the death of my mother had destroyed my childhood and my innocence. That day I lost my faith. Fairy tales and miracles were just stories; the world was unfair, tough, and cruel.

CHAPTER 2

MY MOTHER'S FUNERAL took place the morning after her death. A cart pulled by four horses carried her coffin. The cart was painted gold and black; the horses wore black blinders and were covered with black blankets. Madame Schultz and my father marched behind the cart with my uncle and other friends and relatives. Léon was the only child allowed to accompany the funeral procession. Saby, Denise, and I had to stay home. However, as the cortege passed close to our street, the Corcous came out with us to watch it until it turned and passed out of sight. They held our hands the whole time and took us to their house, where they offered us a hot, comforting meal.

A rabbi came to our home. He said a prayer and tore our undershirts, part of the Jewish tradition of shiva, the week of mourning. During that week, we sat on the floor to eat our meals. We were not allowed to put salt on our eggs or dry our hands after washing them. Denise wore a black dress, and each of us wore a black band around one arm. Dad asked us, the three boys, to memorize the Jewish mourner's prayer, the kaddish, so we could recite it rapidly and keep up with the rabbis. The sight of my father and his three sons reciting the kaddish by heart must have touched many in the congregation of the Camp de Cesar synagogue during the High Holidays.

We struggled without our mother. Mrs. Corcou treated us kindly and fed us whenever we were at her house. Denise continued to attend the English Academy; after Mom's death, Dad persuaded the school to cut its tuition. My sister also cleaned the house and helped Dad prepare our breakfasts. Léon worked at Agami. Saby and I continued to attend the Aghion School. Aunt Pauline volunteered to help, but she was not well enough, hindered by her weight, rheumatism, and diabetes. She had difficulty walking and was always breathless when she arrived at our house. It was hard for her to assist us.

Without Mom's supervision, our grades suffered. I returned to school a few days after her funeral, but I did not play as usual with my friends and did not speak a word about my mother's death. During a Hebrew class, when we had to recite a lesson by heart, the teacher called us to his desk one by one. I had not learned it, as I was unaware of the assignment. Just as I feared, the teacher called on me. I stood up in front of him, rubbing my wrist and incapable of pronouncing a single word. The teacher grew quite upset, because I was one of the best students in our class. He stood up and yelled, "I'm going to give you a zero. You are getting bad habits! What happened to you? Tell me." He shook my shoulders furiously, demanding an answer. I looked at him, and with a trembling voice I said: "My mother died last

Saturday." He suddenly stopped; his hands now softly rubbed my shoulders. He had a sad smile on his face, and his eyes were wet with tears. He hugged me, looked at the class, and asserted, "There will be no zeros for anyone today."

In the first weeks after the death of my mother, suicidal thoughts haunted my mind. To chase them away I dashed out into the streets and ran. Running greatly helped me alleviate my frustration and endure the shock of my mother's death. I often went to the Ibrahimieh Sporting Club, next to the Corcous' house, to run on its oval track, which surrounded a basketball court. I was surprised one day to see a young Arab boy also running on the track. This was unusual, because the Greek community owned the club and we always played with Greek children. This boy, Ahmad, was nice. We raced around the track and played soccer and basketball. We had fun challenging each other and rapidly established a good friendship.

One evening, a big bearded man in a white robe and a black turban came up to us. He looked at Ahmad and told him in Arabic, "This boy is a Jew—he is not allowed to be here." Then, staring at me with piercing eyes, the man declared, "This is a Muslim club. You cannot come here anymore."

The Ibrahimieh Sporting Club, as I later found out, had been sold to the Muslim Brotherhood, an extremist group. Along with the loss of my mother and my faith, I discovered the painful feeling of being discriminated against by an adult because of my religion.

I felt angry with and disappointed in Ahmad. Why did he just stand there while this man chased me out of the club?

Ahmad could have insisted that he wanted to play with me. I would certainly have done that for a friend.

* * *

As time passed, Mom's absence weighed on us even more heavily, especially on Denise, who was entering puberty and needed motherly care and advice. Aunt Pauline could not help her. Although she had been living in Alexandria for years, Aunt Pauline was still just like the people of Chania, where she had grown up. Like my father and other relatives from that part of the world, she was extremely superstitious. She would spit and say, *Pou, pou, pou, mati na mi se piassi* ("May the evil eye not catch you"). She would not allow us to swing our feet when we were sitting in her house, because doing so brought bad luck. We were asked not to shake keys or leave scissors open, because doing so would surely bring disruption to the household.

Aunt Pauline also had a paralyzing fear of mice. She would panic if she saw even a picture of a mouse. Screaming that she was going to faint, she would shake all over if anyone so much as said the word "mouse." As children often do, we teased her sadistically just to see her frightened face. When we would say, "Aunt Pauline, we saw a mouse under your couch," she would scream, cover her eyes with one hand, and lift her feet off the floor. We laughed, of course, not realizing how debilitating and uncontrollable that fear was. We were so cruel.

Because we had a skating rink across the street, Denise could practice often. With time she improved her roller skating and figure skating dramatically. People applauded her, especially the British and French soldiers, who treated her as a younger sister. Denisica's skating skills, however, were still at a beginner's level. Since she lived far from the rink, she could not practice as often as Denise could. This skill gap frustrated Denisica.

While visiting our house one day, Aunt Pauline informed Denise that because her mother had died, it was not proper for her to skate with the soldiers. Soon thereafter Aunt Pauline hired a coach to teach Denisica how to roller-skate and figure-skate, and the lessons were held in the skating rink across from our house.

One evening my father came home, grabbed my sister by her arm, picked up a thick round stick in the kitchen, and took her to our bedroom, where he brutally beat her. We were all taken by surprise and watched helplessly. What had she done? My sister sobbed and screamed herself hoarse. As he beat her, Dad demanded, "Where have you been going? What did you do with those British soldiers?" Denise was sobbing and repeating that she had done nothing wrong. Her screams were filling the house. I was infuriated and could not watch anymore. I had to stop him. I ran to the kitchen and returned with a hammer, prepared to strike my father's legs. By the time I came back, though, Dad had broken the stick on my sister's back. I threw the hammer at his feet; he looked at me and walked away without saying a word. Denise lay crying on the floor.

My father thought Denise had lost her virginity: it turned out that Aunt Pauline, while visiting our house to do laundry, had found blood in Denise's underwear and felt obliged to tell my father about it. She added suspiciously that Denise had been going to the skating rink and had been skating with the British soldiers there. Dad was furious. Apparently it did not occur to my aunt or my father that Denise had just gotten her first menstrual period.

Denise could not understand what was going on; she thought she had some kind of shameful illness. She needed to confide in someone, so she decided to talk to her trusted friend Eliane Wahba.

When Denise told Eliane her problem, Eliane summoned her mother and older sister. "You're not sick; you have nothing to be ashamed of. On the contrary, you're very healthy," the women told Denise. "You're just growing up and becoming a young lady." Then Denise understood what was going on with her body and felt well prepared to confront my father and Aunt Pauline, but nothing more was ever said.

* * *

Under the command of General Erwin Rommel, German troops reached the Egyptian border in April of 1941. Because they were not far from Alexandria, my father began talking about moving to Cairo.

One evening while Uncle Vita was visiting, we overheard Dad say that he planned to hire a matchmaker to find him a woman who did not have children of her own and who would agree to marry a widower with four children. Also, she would have to not mind living in Cairo. Beauty was not a requirement; his sole stipulation was that she be kind and caring with his children.

He found a matchmaker, Moussa Asher, a Jewish man who spoke only Arabic. He, his wife, Regina, and her sister Marie were in Alexandria visiting another sister named Bertha Benzimra. Their maiden name had been Shabbat.

Asher informed my father he need not search too far—Asher's sister-in-law Marie fit his requirements perfectly.

Marie Shabbat had recently divorced a man named René Azoulay and had resumed using her maiden name. We learned later that she had a large hernia because of a botched appendectomy, and she could not bear children as a result. She was not beautiful, but she was kind and patient. My father liked her. He knew that Marie Shabbat was the perfect woman for him. My father and Marie met several times in Alexandria and quickly decided to get married. Marie left soon thereafter for Cairo and wrote to my father that she had found an apartment, which she had prepared for us to move into.

The evening before we left our longtime home in the summer of 1941, I went to our garden, where I had imagined so many bold adventures. I gazed at the sky of Alexandria and at the Corcous' house, where I had spent so much of my childhood. Our neighbors were inside, probably in the kitchen.

Earlier that day we had had an emotional farewell. I kissed Mrs. Corcou and gave a hug to Béba. For the first time, she kissed me on my cheek, and we both blushed. I would miss Béba's company, her Greek lessons, and our chats. And, despite all our past skirmishes, I would miss my cousin Denisica.

Songs drifting from a nearby street shook me out of my reverie. The singers were two men trying to sell drinks. Each man carried his drinks, along with plenty of ice, in a large copper container strapped to his body. One sold *aressouss*, a beverage made with licorice. He sang, *Ya aressouss, sheffaa we khameer, el kharoub menak yegheer, ya aressouss* ("O *aressouss*, healthy and tasty, the carob drink is jealous of you, O *aressouss*"). To which the other salesman responded in his tenor voice, *El ta-ta-tamarhendi*, as he touted the virtues of a sour chilled drink made from tamarind. Both drinks were tasty and always refreshing. Yes, I would miss those, too.

"Jacob, where are you?" My heart bounced in my chest. For a second I thought my mother was calling me, as she used to when I was out for a long time. But it was Denise who was looking for me.

* * *

We decided we would call Dad's new wife Tante Marie (Aunt Marie), as there was no chance we would call any other

Our dog, Helwa, and I with (from left) Saby, my father, Tante Marie, Léon, and Denise in the early 1940s

woman Maman, as we used to call Mom when we spoke French with her.

Tante Marie had selected an apartment on the top floor of a three-story building on a crowded, narrow street, Haret Sawares. (*Haret* means "a small, narrow street.") Large cars and trucks had a hard time driving through. We were the only non-Muslims in the area. We had three bedrooms: two connected and a larger one on the other side of the house. In Alexandria the four of us had slept in one bedroom, two in each bed. In the new home we could sleep two in each of the connecting bedrooms. My father and Tante Marie had the separate large room on the other side of the apartment.

Our living room also functioned as a dining room. Tante Marie brought her furniture: a couch, two large chairs, a coffee table, a large round table, and six chairs. We also had an extra room for storage. The only furniture in the storeroom was a table and two chairs that I used when I was doing my homework or listening to Greek music on the radio that Tante Marie had brought with her.

Like our apartment in Alexandria, our new apartment had no shower or tub. For bathing we continued to heat water on a Primus stove. Our biggest disappointment, however, was the toilet: a hole and a faucet with which to clean it. We were shocked. It took us some time to get used to it.

Our building provided an unusual luxury—a *bawab*, a doorman. We lived in a poor section but were proud to have a *bawab* in our building. Our doorman slept in a small wooden room built under the stairs on the ground floor. We never knew his full name; we just called him Ahmad el Bawab. To make extra money he sold ice, sodas, and—as I found out later—beer, when no religious people were around.

Ahmad was a womanizer. He flirted with the neighbors' house cleaners. Even though we were living in a low-income neighborhood, residents could afford to hire servants, who worked for subsistence wages and daily meals. Ahmad and I established a good relationship. He would run errands for us, especially in the evenings, when everyone was too tired to go out. We bought our sodas and ice and occasionally a bottle of beer from him.

* * *

When we got to Cairo, Saby, Denise, and I had to select our schools. Denise chose a French high school, and Saby enrolled in a technical school that specialized in basic mechanical courses. Both left school after one or two years; they were eager to work and gain their independence. My father did not mind, because it helped him financially.

As for me, Tante Marie suggested l'École Cattaui in Daher, our Cairo suburb. The school, which was within walking distance of our house, was also known as the Jewish Community School of Daher. To get there, I walked along the main street, Sakakini Street, which was close to Haret Sawares, the narrow street where we lived. It was named for the wealthy Sakakini Pasha family, who lived in a beautiful mansion, the Sakakini Palace, in the middle of Sakakini Square.

There were two schools adjacent to each other. L'École Cattaui was the private Jewish academy for boys, and Marie Suarez was its counterpart for girls. Two wealthy and prominent Egyptian Jewish families, Cattaui and Suarez, founded the highly regarded academies. Members of both families had a significant influence on Egyptian cultural and economic developments, especially Moise Cattaui Pasha, who held an important position in the Egyptian government. The Jewish community subsidized both schools. The nominal tuition was based on a student's financial resources.

In August of 1941, soon after our arrival in Cairo, Tante Marie and I went to l'École Cattaui. It was a few weeks before the start of the new school year. Monsieur Hayim, the headmaster, who had gray hair and a gentle, inviting face, received us. He was also the math teacher and the only person present at the school that day. He had the authority to accept students, determine the grade level at which they would enter, and even negotiate the tuition to be paid.

All our conversations were in French. He gave me a French text to read and asked me several questions, testing my French vocabulary and spelling. He then gave me a few math problems, which I completed with ease. I must have done well, because he told us that I would be the youngest student in the class. Then, seemingly as an afterthought, he said, "By the way, the main language at our school is Arabic."

Surprised and disappointed, I asked, "All the courses?"

"Well, we also teach French and Hebrew, but math, geography, and history are all in Arabic," he replied with a smile.

I was far from fluent in Arabic, because we never spoke it among ourselves in Alexandria. Sensing my disappointment and concern, Monsieur Hayim assured me: "Don't worry, you will soon learn it; it will be very easy." He immediately sought the information he needed to register me. When he asked about my father's job, Tante Marie's face grew despondent, and in a low, tight voice, she said that her husband had no steady job and no fixed salary. Our financial situation was precarious. She was impressive and convincing. Monsieur Hayim asked her to pay just a nominal amount of tuition, and registration was completed.

Before we left, he asked me if I had a nickname. I told him that everyone called me Jacob. I must have grimaced as I said it, because he then said, "If you want to, we can change your name right here and now. Do you have a name you prefer?" I answered that I preferred to be called Jacques. He said, "Jacques, like Jean-Jacques Rousseau?" Jean-Jacques Rousseau, I knew, was a French writer and philosopher; like me, he had lost his mother at a young age. From then on everyone called me Jacques except my father, who called me Jacob all his life.

My first few weeks at l'École Cattaui were difficult. I had no friends, and I was not an outgoing kid who found it easy to establish new relationships. It took me a while to adjust to the new school and to speaking Arabic. Our Arabic language professor, Effendi Taha ("effendi" is a form of address used for a highly educated man in Arab countries), volunteered to tutor me after class. By the end of my first term at Cattaui, I had improved noticeably, and Effendi Taha was proud of me. The next year I was doing so well in Arabic that I was first in the class. I did well in grammar and writing, too. My vocabulary was not rich, but I compensated with a creative writing style. Despite all my efforts, however, I could not get rid of my foreign accent.

I now speak seven languages with various degrees of fluency, but always with a pronounced foreign accent. I have lived in many countries, and after living for more than forty years in the United States, I feel I am American. But when people listen to me speak, they often ask where I am from. I always take a while to answer, because in truth I do not know.

Sometimes people say, "Well, the answer is easy. You are from the place you were born—where was that?"

I sometimes hesitate and reply, "Egypt."

"So you are Egyptian."

No; I do not feel Egyptian. Even the Egyptians did not consider me one of them; I was a *khawaga*, a term, indicating respect, reserved for people of European descent. The Egyptian authorities denied me citizenship and deemed me an *apatride*, which meant that I had no *patrie*, no country—I was stateless. To avoid being called Egyptian, and to avoid having to give lengthy explanations, I would usually lie and say that I was born in Greece. Even though I had never lived there, I was raised as a Greek by a Greek father. But when I was in Greece or among Greeks, if someone asked me about my origins, I would answer that I was originally from France, thinking that being the son of a mother who had lived in France would justify it.

But now that many years have passed, I no longer need to lie or use subterfuge. I have adopted the most convenient answer, which I give without further explanation: "I'm American. I was born in Egypt, but I'm not Egyptian." That leaves the questioner even more perplexed.

* * *

Although most of our classes were conducted in Arabic, the director of our school, Roger Moline, was a retired French general who did not speak Arabic. Authoritarian and inflexible, he applied strict military discipline to the school. He dressed in a suit and tie, and he wore the medal of the Legion of Honor on his lapel. He walked with a ramrod-straight back and carried a baton under his arm.

Every morning we lined up in the courtyard. Monsieur Moline stood with our gym teacher, Effendi Aziz, a short, lithe, energetic man who had been a gymnast in his youth. With his whistle Effendi Aziz ordered us to line up, run in place, do jumping jacks, and perform a few stretching exercises. He then introduced Monsieur Moline, who would ask one of us to step up and recite part of the Jewish morning prayer. As soon as it ended, we all rushed up the stairs to our classes.

We did not like Monsieur Moline. He never smiled and was always trying to catch somebody doing something wrong. We used to call him Teez El Erd (monkey's ass) because his cheeks were always extremely red, like the rear end of a baboon. Monsieur Moline hated sports, and he considered them a waste of time.

The school courtyard had a basketball hoop at each end. The playing area, which had no marked lines, was in bad shape. On rare occasions, when we knew for sure that Monsieur Moline had gone home or had an off-campus meeting to attend, we stayed after class and organized basketball or soccer games.

For those games, we all depended on a student by the name of Mizrahi, a Karaite Jew, to bring the ball. (The Karaites are an old Jewish sect that rejects rabbinic tradition and accepts only the authority of the Old Testament.) Mizrahi was the wealthiest kid in our school. He brought a leather basketball that he would share with us, but only if we allowed him to play the whole time. Since he owned the ball, and since none of us could afford one, we had to accept his condition, even though he was an awful, uncoordinated player.

Initially, I remained quite distant from the other students in my class during that first year. But two boys, Elie Masri and Maurice Samama, made a special effort to put me at ease. Both were two years older and had attended the school since first grade.

For some reason they sympathized with me and must have been moved by my loneliness. They included me in their conversations and exclusive circle. Maurice was the *fetewa*, the tough guy, of the class and influenced the rest of his group. I think he genuinely wanted to help a newcomer, but I also believe that he thought I might be a good fighter because I was in good shape, and Maurice liked to fight.

Elie Masri was the first among us to leave school; he needed to work, and after I had been there for a year he found a job as an assistant salesman at Orosdi-Back, a well-known Cairo department store. Maurice followed a couple of years later, after obtaining his Egyptian lower-school certificate. A government-owned company that produced jute bags hired him because the manager, a Jewish man, was related to Maurice's mother.

As for me, I stayed in school; I wanted to continue my studies and was determined to learn as much as I could. I knew that, thanks to Tante Marie's negotiation skills, my studies did not cost much, so I could continue. My dream was to become a doctor. To me doctors were knowledgeable, respected, and helped people who were suffering. Doctors were wealthy, their families were never short of money, and their children did not go to bed without food. So I stayed in school.

With Elie Masri (left) and Maurice Samama in 1949

Elie, Maurice, and I remained friends even after they left school to go to work. They had enough money to go out every weekend and even to eat in a fancy restaurant on occasion. I avoided them for quite a while, but they kept insisting that I accompany them on their Saturday evening outings. They knew I could not afford it. I finally realized that they really just wanted me to be with them. Elie in particular would buy movie tickets in advance, and most of the time he refused reimbursement. In the end I did not mind; I knew he was happy to pay my way and that he enjoyed my company as much as I enjoyed his.

* * *

In the mid-1940s my classmates and I started holding regular after-school basketball practices with the assistance of Effendi Aziz. The Cairo basketball federation had, for some years, sponsored a tournament for the schools. Effendi Aziz kept telling us that if we practiced and got good enough, we could play in that tournament. We were excited and motivated. We agreed that I would coach and be the captain of the team if we entered. After one of our practices, Effendi Aziz gathered us in the school's courtyard. He told us we were ready and that he would ask Monsieur Moline to authorize him to form the Cattaui basketball team. Then, looking at me, he added, "You can continue to take care of the team, can't you?" I looked at the players, and they all nodded.

A few days later Effendi Aziz took me aside. Monsieur Moline had turned down his request and was adamantly opposed to having the school sponsor a basketball team. According to Monsieur Moline, basketball would distract the students from their studies. I did not say anything. I left Effendi Aziz and resumed playing with my teammates. I knew Monsieur Moline was completely wrong. I was not about to accept his no as a final answer.

A few days later I called a meeting and told my teammates what had happened. All agreed that we could do nothing to make Monsieur Moline change his mind. I then suggested we take drastic action: "The only way we can get the school board's attention is to go on strike." Everyone stared in shock. Student strikes, common at Egyptian schools and universities at the time, usually involved political, religious, and social causes. But the idea seemed unimaginable in such a conservative and strictly disciplined school as l'École Cattaui.

"We have always criticized the schools that went on strike," said one player.

"You're right," I answered. "However, it's not the same." I argued at length that our strike was different. Our cause was one of justice. Sports did not adversely affect studies or discipline, as Monsieur Moline claimed. What other recourse did we have? We all knew that officials would take a dim view of a strike at our school and would certainly impose harsh disciplinary action in response. On the other hand, this was the only way to bring the matter to the attention of school board members and the school's benefactors in the Jewish community. We had to go over Monsieur Moline's head. I ended my long argument with two questions. "How much do we really want to have the team? And are we ready to take such a risk?"

A few moments of silence followed. Then a player solemnly said: "It's true. We are all longing to have a basketball team, so we will have to take some risk in order to make it happen."

Slowly they all started to agree. The strike was the only way we could express our frustrations. That evening we prepared anonymous notes for distribution to the student body: these notes would explain the reason for the strike and call a general meeting to be held at a location far from school. Early the next morning, when nobody was likely to notice, we placed these notes on each student's desk.

The strike took place the next day. When the students assembled on an empty field in Abbassieh, a suburb of

Cairo, I explained the reason for the strike and gave everyone the choice to stay or go to school. Only a few students decided to leave us.

When those students returned to school, Monsieur Moline threatened to expel them if they did not reveal the names of the strike instigators. Pressed by such intimidations, the students ratted us out. Monsieur Moline's suspicion that I was the strike leader was rapidly confirmed.

In response, Monsieur Moline suspended the members of our basketball team and its supporters until the year-end exams, which were scheduled for around two months later. Anyone who failed would be expelled from school, and Monsieur Moline was convinced that our entire basketball team would fail because we wouldn't be able to attend class.

We decided that we would not lament the consequences of our strike and rapidly established our objective: each of us, without exception, must pass the year-end exams with good grades. We met daily in a nearby park and studied for the length of a school day. Using our schoolbooks, we had to understand and review all past courses as well as learn new material. We elected the student who was strongest in each subject to act as a teacher and give out homework assignments.

We met every single day during those two months. I suspect that most families thought their children were at school. I know that my family did not have a clue about what was going on. When exam time arrived, we were all well prepared and entered our classroom with our chins up. The other students expected us to act repentant, but we gave Monsieur Moline a defiant look. He must have ordered that the exams be graded promptly: only a few days afterward, we were asked to assemble in a conference room to hear the results.

Our group had the best grades in the class. We could not contain our joy and excitement. Most of the astonished teachers, especially Effendi Aziz, were happy, barely suppressing their smiles. Monsieur Moline was visibly frustrated; his plan had not worked. However, the rules he had established could not be altered. He had to comply. Nevertheless he convinced the school board that, as the leader of the group, I deserved a harsher punishment. I had to be interrogated and scolded and maybe even expelled.

A few days later, I was asked to meet with representatives of the school's board of directors. I was escorted to a conference room that students were not usually allowed to enter. I saw Monsieur Moline sitting with four other men behind a long table on a high platform. Monsieur Moline explained that the men were members of the Jewish community and would ask me questions about the strike. A long silence followed. Finally one man spoke up. "Monsieur Sardas," he said. "During the many years of operation at l'École Moise Cattaui, there has never been a strike." Then he added, "There is no way the school will allow such an event to take place again." Monsieur Moline stood up and pointed his finger at me and declared, "You are the one who provoked this horrible event."

I allowed some time to pass, and then, looking up at them, I asked permission to speak. I placed my hands behind my back and told them my side of the story: "Messieurs, I believe in sports. Sports do not have a negative impact on studies; on the contrary, *Mens sana in corpore sano*" ("A sound mind in a sound body"). I knew that my statements impressed my interlocutors, because they looked at each other and exchanged a few words with Monsieur Moline.

I continued, "We accepted the punishment applied by the board and by Monsieur Moline, and, as you probably know, we scored excellent grades on the final exams. We had the courage to make our voices heard. What the school did, though, with some of our classmates—frightening them to the point where they had to betray their colleagues—is worse: it teaches them to become traitors." I stopped. My heart pounded as I wondered whether I had gone too far. I figured that if I were expelled, I would leave school with the satisfaction of having expressed my feelings about Monsieur Moline's dictatorial regime. A long pause followed. The group whispered among themselves. Finally the men asked me to wait outside. The committee would deliberate and decide my fate.

Anxious and worried, I waited on a bench and rubbed the birthmark on my wrist. It dawned on me that this might be my last day at school. All my dreams for higher education might be about to disappear. After what seemed an eternity, the men came out of the conference room. Only one man stayed in the room and called me in. I learned later that it was Dr. Yallouz, a well-known personality in Cairo. He had a doctoral degree in Egyptian history, and he had perfectly mastered the Arabic language. He was an active member of the Jewish community and at one time held a prestigious job as director of the world-renowned Egyptian Museum in Cairo. He said: "We've decided to let you stay in school. If you create a similar incident, you'll be expelled on the spot. Do you understand?" I nodded. He then put his arm on my shoulder and said, "We've also agreed that the school will have a basketball team next year. Monsieur Moline will discuss this matter with your gym teacher." It was difficult for me to contain my joy. I took Dr. Yallouz's hand and kept shaking it and thanking him at the same time.

When he saw me the next morning, Monsieur Moline came to me and said, "Sardas, you'll become a bum when you grow up—you'll spend most of your life in prison." Two days later, after our morning prayer, Effendi Aziz announced that Monsieur Moline had decided to form a basketball team. The whole school cheered and applauded. They knew what we had done to get approval to form a team. The pariahs became heroes. We all enjoyed a euphoric moment of victory.

* * *

A few days after we returned to school in September of 1944, we received our uniforms: dark blue shorts and light blue-and-white shirts with ÉCOLE CATTAUI printed in dark blue on the back. We had to provide our own sneakers and socks, but the school offered us two brand-new official basketballs, which we considered a special gift. The school did not agree to hire a coach, however, and we did not insist on having one.

We practiced almost every day after class. We had no experience playing an official game against other teams; we always played against each other. We had no adult support except that of Effendi Aziz, who stayed with us all the time, but he could not be of any technical help because he had never played the game and had no experience with basketball rules. We had no strategic setups for either offense or defense. All we had were motivation and enthusiasm.

When we received our game schedule for the season, we saw to our dismay that our first match would be against the Lycée Franco-Égyptien, the undefeated and uncontested champions of the previous season. We were intimidated and disheartened. The game would take place on a Saturday afternoon at the YMCA.

Our team arrived for the matchup two hours earlier than our opponents did, and it was the first time any of us had used a locker room. We had played on our school court in our school clothes and changed only our shoes. Now we wore our new uniforms and were set to play an official game in front of a large audience, both for the first time. Having a scoreboard and a time clock, as well as two referees officiating the game, were also intimidating new experiences.

After only a few minutes of play it was clear that we were heading for an overwhelming defeat. We were nervous, impatient, and had no strategies for confronting a well-orchestrated team. Our performance proved far below our skills and capabilities. We lost by a large margin, something like 50–2.

Our opponents laughed and mocked us. I was disheartened and stayed in the middle of the court with my head bowed. The captain of the opposing team walked up beside me. I thought he was going to shake my hand after our defeat. Instead he leaned toward me and whispered, "You are a bunch of losers!"

I didn't react; I had only one thought in mind. I wanted to talk to my teammates before they went home discouraged. I pleaded with them to stay a few more minutes. I looked at them and said: "This was a horrible disaster." They looked at me with worn-out and confused faces, as if to say, "You wanted us to stay so you could state the obvious?"

Their expressions struck me as funny, and I could not contain my laughter. After a few seconds of hesitation, they all laughed with me. "It was indeed a complete collapse," I went on. "This is our first and worst game—and this defeat may be the best thing that could have happened to us. We will have to play better from now on. You know, if we work hard and stick together, soon we'll be able to beat this team."

I could see my teammates listening and absorbing my words. "Determination and teamwork will be the key to our future success. Let's go and take a good hot shower to wash away our defeat," I said and headed to the locker room.

This was also the first time I had had a shower. The hot water was relaxing and helped me overcome my fatigue and frustration. I stayed a long time, letting the hot water flow over my head and body. What a good invention—I did not have to heat the water as we did at home. Dad, of course, had warned us that showers could make us susceptible to pneumonia. This first shower was so enjoyable that I felt as if I were committing a sin.

The following Monday morning Effendi Aziz announced the results of the game to everyone in the courtyard without mentioning the score. He just reported that our team had fought valiantly but lost to the best team in the league. I could not help but notice a slight smile on Monsieur Moline's face.

* * *

My family was unaware of my sports activities. My father did not get involved in my studies and did not know that I played basketball. My brothers and my sister were busy taking care of their own lives, and I was pretty much left on my own.

I exercised and played sports without my father's knowledge for a long time. For him, exercise was a way to expose the body to infectious diseases. He believed that taking a bath and going out afterward was a sure way to get sick. Cold weather was another cause of illness: we had to wear several layers of clothing under our coats during the mild Egyptian winters. My father even forced us to cover our chests with newspapers for extra protection against the cold.

One evening he confronted me when I got home. A friend of his had just told him that he had seen me playing basketball at the YMCA. Shocked and angry, Dad launched into a long tirade about how sports were bad for my health. "You have to stop doing those crazy things. You're not built for these kinds of activities!" he yelled.

I was upset and could hardly contain my anger, but I could not interrupt him. When he stopped, I yelled: "Dad, I know you want to protect us. But I like sports and will not quit! Cattaui has a basketball team now, and we are participating in a tournament. I am the captain of the team, and I am a good player. I play sports, perspire, take showers, and feel great."

My father grew unusually quiet. My determination and my clandestine participation in sports surprised him. I also sensed that he was proud that his son was the captain of the team. Taking advantage of his silence, I continued in a softer voice, "I've been practicing sports for a long time, and, as you well know, all along I have not gotten sick or caught pneumonia."

He stood up and placed his hands on a wooden cabinet. "Let's touch wood." Then he smiled and asked, "When can I come and watch one of your games?"

The team was training with great intensity after our first defeat. Our loss had indeed motivated us to improve and to play at a higher level. We even started winning a few games. But we still remained far behind in our league. Dad came to watch one evening, and we were lucky enough to win that game. He came to the court while we celebrated our victory, and in front of all the players and officials, he put his hand on my head to bless me in Hebrew. Although I was somewhat embarrassed, I let him do it. I knew he was happy and proud, and I did not want to spoil his moment of enjoyment.

At the end of one of our games, an official of the Maccabi Daher Club approached me and said he wanted to recruit players from our school. Maccabi Daher fielded one of the best basketball teams in Egypt; they had several famous players, notably the five Harari brothers. I soon joined the club and started training. Some coaches were players from Maccabi's top teams who volunteered to participate in our development. I soon established a good relationship with one of their starters, Victor Shabbott, who was athletic and possessed excellent basketball skills.

The Egyptian Basketball Federation was in charge of the official basketball tournaments among various leagues. The top league, with the best basketball players, was the most popular. Fans of all nationalities followed their games passionately. Every team in the top league represented a different ethnic group. The Maccabi team represented the Jewish community; Keravnos ("thunder" in Greek), the Greek community; Ararat, the Armenians; Palestra, the Italians; and a Maronite team represented the Syrian and Lebanese communities. The Egyptian police and army teams mainly represented the Muslims. Although it mostly served Christians, the YMCA was used by a mixture of nationalities and religions.

Victor Shabbott came to watch one of our school games at the YMCA. Afterward he suggested that he come to our school to work with us during our practices. His assistance proved invaluable. We started winning more games. We grew well acquainted with the various strategic plays and labeled them with numbers. We won the quarterfinals and then the semifinals. In the finals we were to meet the team that had humiliated us the year before, the team from the Lycée Franco-Égyptien.

As soon as the game started, our opponents found themselves playing a team completely different from the one they had trounced a year earlier. We had gotten much better while they had stagnated—at least, that was how we felt. We scored almost every time we had the ball, and our defense worked even more efficiently. The game was tight and memorable. The lead changed hands often until the last five minutes, when our team summoned all its energy and determination. We won. Our dream had finally come true. We were the champions.

After the prayer in the school courtyard the next morning, Effendi Aziz held the silver championship trophy and announced with great fanfare that the school had won the basketball tournament. "L'École Cattaui is the champion," he said, barely able to contain his tears. "And here are our heroes." With Monsieur Moline standing at his side, Effendi Aziz called each player to join him and had us face all the students, who were lined up as usual. "And here is our captain," he said as he called my name. He handed me the trophy and asked me to hold it aloft and show it to the students. He then signaled that I should hand it to Monsieur Moline, which I did. After a brief hesitation Monsieur Moline shook my hand and said, "Congratulations." I barely had time to respond before the whole school exploded with cheers, whistles, and applause.

I harbored a profound passion for basketball; it offered me a way to escape my family's financial problems and avoid depression. I also worked hard at my studies. Although Monsieur Moline became more tolerant of school sports after we won the championship, he continued to keep a vigilant eye on my academic performance and behavior, but I did not give him the satisfaction of finding fault with me. I was still getting some of the best grades in my class. I did well in Arabic grammar and in history, geography, and math, all taught in Arabic. In French I was one of the top students, if not the top student, in my class.

Winning the championship raised our school's profile with its benefactors and other members of the Jewish community. Now we could see younger students playing basketball during recess. The championship also raised my profile at school in a remarkable and somewhat surprising way, as I came to find out.

One evening Tante Marie returned home from a visit to friends who lived in our neighborhood. As soon as she entered our house, she asked my father, "Do you know what they call your son Jacob at school? They call him Jacques Sardas—*el shaguiy*." She pronounced my first and last name together as if they formed just one name: *Jaxardas*. *El shaguiy* in Arabic means something like a combination of "the hero" and "the kid." The Lone Ranger, Zorro, and various American cowboys were each called *el shaguiy* in Egypt.

Although I was surprised to learn of my nickname, I was, I must admit, quite proud of it. By calling me Jaxardas, El Shaguiy, the kids were dubbing me a sort of Robin Hood of the playground, someone who helped people, protected the weak, and imposed justice.

* * *

After we moved to Cairo, Léon's employer in Alexandria, the brokerage house Agami, sent an emissary to our home to offer him a job in Cairo. We were all quite proud, because the offer proved that he was smart and skillful. Léon worked there for a couple of years and then left for a better job at the Banque Belge du Caire. He made that change on the advice of his friend Victor Abada, whom he had met at Agami. Victor Abada worked full-time at the bank but was a part-time accountant for Agami.

Our financial situation in Cairo was far better than it had been in Alexandria. Dad was selling more fabric. Léon was earning his own money. But oddly enough family life was more contentious than it had been in Alexandria. Most fights were about money issues between my father and Léon. Because Léon had the best-paid job in our family, my father wanted him to contribute more to the household expenses.

Dad used every conceivable tactic to get more financial help from Léon. He ran after him and yelled at him; he begged from him and insulted him; he threatened to not let him in the house. Dad even went as far as to search Léon's pockets while he was sleeping. Léon, however, hid his money in his shoes, his socks, and other places where he was sure Dad would not find it. Dad then discovered a more effective way to extract money from my brother. He would go to Léon's office at the Banque Belge and would threaten Léon with a scandalous confrontation in front of all his clients, colleagues, and supervisors. Léon would fold and give the money to our father. In a certain way this was not dissimilar to the way Léon, as a kid, would get extra pocket money when Dad was busy betting on horse races in Alexandria.

* * *

During my third year at Cattaui, we learned that we were getting a new French teacher. He was Dutch, and since I do not recall his name, I will call him Mr. Van Der Huysen. He was an excellent teacher and a good psychologist. He was impartial and handled his students according to their skills but always challenged each of us to strive for a higher level.

He encouraged me to develop my creative writing skills and gave me additional assignments by asking me to write papers describing people and places I knew. He was so impressed with one of my papers that he read it aloud to our class while Monsieur Moline was visiting us. Our teacher had not mentioned who wrote it.

As Mr. Van Der Huysen was reading, Monsieur Moline kept looking at my classmate Pierre, whose bookish ways and pure Parisian accent had long made him the star of French class. Certain that Pierre wrote the paper, Monsieur

Moline was smiling broadly. Then he applauded, walked to Pierre's desk, and exclaimed, "It is marvelous! Very well written!" At that moment Mr. Van Der Huysen came to my desk and handed me the paper: "Yes, Jacques, it is really well written. Bravo!"

Monsieur Moline was surprised and not at all pleased that I was making significant progress in French and getting better grades than Pierre. And Pierre, not used to playing second fiddle, became bitter and jealous. Although I was proud of my achievement, I did not like to see him depressed. I decided to improve our relationship. We exchanged notes and talked more often during recess. I even encouraged him to practice basketball with us. We studied together many times, to the delight of our teacher, who challenged us to advance to a level far above the rest of our class.

Mr. Van Der Huysen called both of us to his office one day during our last year of lower school, 1944, and told us we were ready to pass the Certificat d'Études Primaires, supervised by the French education commission in Egypt. Because l'École Cattaui was an Arabic school that also taught French and Hebrew, the French Certificat d'Études Primaires was not required. However, Mr. Van Der Huysen thought that Pierre and I were sufficiently advanced to pass the exam. He said, "You'll have no problem—I'm sure of it." Then, looking sadly at us, he told us that he would be leaving his job at the end of our school year. He shook our hands and said, *Votre directeur ne connaît pas le fair play. Il ne croit pas au give and take* ("Your director does not know fair play; he does not believe in give and take"). He did not need to elaborate on the reason for his departure. I had learned long before how unfair Monsieur Moline could be.

Indeed, Pierre and I passed our Certificat d'Études Primaires. Afterward, when I saw Mr. Van Der Huysen at school, I told him how easy the French exam was. Then we embraced, knowing that we might not meet again. When he noticed the sadness on my face, he said, "This is your last year in lower school, and my departure should not be so bad because you will also leave the school in a few months." He stopped because his voice was revealing his own sadness. To regain his composure he said, "Now get ready for your final exams, and study hard." He then turned, walked away, and added, "*Bonne chance*, Jacques!" That was the last time I saw him. He certainly proved to be one of the most important people in my life. He helped me to persevere, to believe in myself, and to give free rein to my imagination.

* * *

L'École Cattaui's lower school ended with what we called in Arabic *al shihada al ibtidaheya*, the Egyptian lower-school certificate. The exams were supervised by the Egyptian board of education. Because they did not have the means or the desire to continue their studies after passing the lower-school certificate exams, most of the school's students, whose studies had been subsidized by the Jewish community, got low-level jobs in banks, insurance companies, department stores, and other businesses owned by prominent Jewish families. Few went to Egyptian high schools to obtain the Arabic baccalaureate, called *al shihada al sanaweya*, which required another five years of study.

Most of the seats in Egyptian high schools were reserved for students related to government dignitaries or for wealthy people who paid high tuition. For those who lacked the necessary financial resources, the only way to enroll in high school was to earn good grades. Students could obtain a scholarship if they passed all subjects and achieved high enough grades to be ranked among the top students nationwide. So I needed every ounce of good luck that Mr. Van Der Huysen had wished me before his departure.

A few weeks before our final exams, Monsieur Moline came to our class with Dr. Yallouz. He explained that the Jewish community had decided to start a high school within the Cattaui school building, and we were to be the pioneers. Our class would expand the high school as we advanced. It would be complete, with five classes, by the time we passed the exams for our baccalaureate.

Monsieur Moline mentioned that the new high school would follow the same admission policy as other Egyptian high schools. Only the top students would earn scholarships. Everyone else could attend if they could pay tuition. This important decision by the Jewish community meant that fewer students would have to give up their studies and go to work after finishing lower school. To realize my dream of becoming a doctor, I had to earn high enough grades to obtain a scholarship. It was a tough challenge, but anything less than that for me would mean failure.

In the past I had managed to advance to the next grade without having to study much. I handled my homework in a few minutes while at school or while having dinner at home. But now I would compete for the top level of academic achievement against students from all over the country. During the few weeks remaining before the exams, I studied rigorously and began an intensive schedule that lasted way past midnight. I used the quiet extra room in our apartment, which proved an invaluable haven.

One night I got an unexpected visit from a daring gray mouse. At first I tried to chase him and even kill him, but he hid in a hole between the door and the wall. A few minutes later he pointed his nose out of the hole. As he gained courage, he would come closer to me. After a few evenings like this, the mouse became my companion. He did not miss an evening; we became inseparable. I called him Mickey, and I did not tell anyone about him. We both concentrated on my getting ready for the great challenge.

The evening before our exams I gave Mickey a little piece of cheese and said good-bye. I did not want him to become too confident about coming out of his hole and trying to be friendly to other people, who would certainly try to kill him. I stopped going into the storeroom at night. I hoped that Mickey would go to another place when he couldn't find me. When I went back after a few weeks, he did not emerge, and I did not see Mickey again.

I passed my Egyptian lower-school exams with honors, ranking among the top 7 percent of students nationwide. I had obtained grades way above the scores that qualified me for a high school scholarship. It was an important event in my life. Without these grades I could not have continued my studies; I might have become a bum, as Monsieur Moline predicted. But now I could continue my high school studies at l'École Cattaui. Monsieur Moline was wrong after all.

During the years I attended l'École Cattaui, I paid little attention to the war. I knew in broad terms what was happening, but I was not interested in learning more. Dad had proved prescient in moving us to Cairo. Although the war in the desert came within forty miles of Alexandria before Bernard Montgomery, the Allied troop commander, defeated Rommel in the crucial battle of El Alamein in late 1942, the war affected Cairo mostly by making it more cosmopolitan than ever. As the headquarters for Allied forces in North Africa, the city was bursting with soldiers from dozens of nations as well as European refugees and countless spies.

The year of my exams, 1944, marked the dismantling of the Axis forces. The Americans invaded Normandy, Britain liberated Greece, and the Italians had already capitulated—it was the beginning of the end of Hitler's reign of terror.

* * *

By 1945 both Saby and Denise were working full-time—Denise at the Salon Vert, a fabric store, and Saby at Maison Cicurel, the most famous upscale department store in Cairo. My brothers and sister now earned enough to cover their personal expenses. I was busy with my studies and my sports activities. I became an avid reader of French books. As soon as I arrived home after a basketball game or other physical exercise, I would have a bite to eat, grab a book, and go to bed to read. My reading included authors of classic literature such as Proust, Hugo, Dumas, Zola, Balzac, Corneille, Racine, Molière, Verlaine, and many more.

To figure out the meaning of many unfamiliar words, I used the *Petit Larousse* dictionary frequently and kept it under my bed for easy access. Through my reading, I developed my imagination and enriched my French vocabulary. On winter nights I would keep a lit Primus stove near my bed. Its monotonous humming gave me a special feeling of security, comfort, and warmth. It also had a soporific effect and created for me a lethargic state that transported me to the adventures of the characters I read about.

Late one night I was awakened by a commotion in Léon and Saby's bedroom, which was next to the one Denise and I shared. The lights were on, and my father and Tante Marie were busy placing cold pads on Saby's and Léon's foreheads. Both had high fevers and were complaining about excruciating headaches. My father gave my brothers hot tea and aspirin; he was going to stay with them until they fell asleep. "I'll take care of them," he said. "Tomorrow they'll feel better."

The next morning the fevers and the headaches were worse. Saby and Léon were subjected to Dad's usual treatment—chicken broth, purging, hot tea, aspirin, and suction cups—but they showed no sign of improvement. On the contrary, their fevers were getting alarmingly higher, and the skin all over their bodies had erupted with red spots. "I'll have to call a doctor," Dad announced.

Early that afternoon he told us he had been able to persuade a Greek doctor to come to our home after office hours. The doctor arrived late at night. He was pale and out of breath from climbing the stairs. I was disappointed and surprised to see him in such bad shape. I thought doctors were supposed to be fit and healthy.

My father did not waste time. He embraced the doctor and thanked him profusely for his kindness. Then he showed him to my brothers' bedroom. After a short examination the doctor came out and asked my father to show him where he could wash his hands. While he was drying them, he said, "They have smallpox, both of them." He stopped to watch the effect of this announcement on my father's face. My father was so desperate that I feared he would faint. The doctor went on: "I can see that you know how serious this is. It is an epidemic and highly contagious illness, and all doctors have to declare such cases to the public health department, which will order you to take them to a public hospital that specializes in contagious diseases. It's not a good place to be."

My father was speechless, holding his hands in a begging position. "Don't worry," the doctor said. "I do not intend to report them; I don't want to kill them by sending them there. However, you have to promise me that you are going to follow my instructions. First of all, nobody outside this household can know; second, do not allow anyone to have any contact with them. It would be a disaster." My father hastened to say, "Don't worry, Doctor, we'll do exactly what you have said. We promise."

"Good, because if more of your children catch it, they will all be taken away from your house; you will be fined, and I will lose my license." The doctor continued: "Keep a bottle of rubbing alcohol in your sons' bedroom. Whenever you and your wife come in and out, you have to clean your hands. It's very important—do you understand?"

The doctor did not wait for more reassurance; he went back to my brothers' bedroom and told them to be careful not to let any of us touch them. Above all, the doctor told them not to scratch their red spots. He prescribed a solution and told them to use cotton balls to apply it to the spots without rubbing. "This way, you will alleviate the itching and minimize the scars that usually result from this disease."

All of us religiously followed the doctor's instructions. He came to our house almost every day that first week. After a while his visits became less frequent, until my brothers had fully recovered. He embraced them the last time he came, telling them how happy he was that they were in good health. Then he said with a large smile, "You're lucky—there are no scars on your faces!" My brothers soon resumed their daily activities and went back to work.

The doctor died a few months later. His widow told Dad that her husband had an incurable tumor and that he knew it was terminal. However, he continued working and taking care of his patients until he had to be hospitalized. When Dad brought us the news, we were sad, as though the doctor were part of our family. He then told us that the doctor, despite all his visits, had refused to accept any payment.

* * *

"What's your name? And how old are you?" asked a man with a deep voice who was standing behind me. We had just finished a basketball game at the YMCA. The palm of his hand rested on my shoulder; I did not know whether the gesture was to reassure me or to hold me so that I would not walk away from him. I turned around. "Jacques Sardas; I'm seventeen," I answered as I assessed the short, stocky middle-aged man. Then I asked, "Why?"

He said his name was Zaccot, he owned a fitness center, and he wanted me to join his club. Cairo did not have many fitness centers with modern equipment and certified trainers back then. The name Zaccot was well known.

I stared at Monsieur Zaccot, unable to react to his invitation. I was surprised and embarrassed because my parents could not afford it. He must have guessed what was going through my mind, because he immediately said that I would be able to use the facilities at no charge and as often and for as long as I wanted. "We'll be glad to have you in our center," he said. He handed me a card and left. I could not believe what had just happened to me. I smiled all the way home.

And so I became an habitué of the Zaccot fitness center. Although I was involved in several sports, I had not worked out with weights; my strength and resistance exercises were limited to push-ups, pull-ups, sit-ups, and the like. Now I was training with weights at the fitness center whenever I had a free hour or two. I enjoyed going there. My muscles were developing rapidly, and I was attaining results that were noticeable to my family and friends.

After a few months a trainer told me that Monsieur Zaccot wanted to see me. I found a well-dressed couple in his office. I guessed they were the parents of the slim young man with a pale face who was sitting with them. Zaccot put his arm around my shoulder and presented me to them: "I want you to meet Jacques Sardas; he has been training with us for less than six months. When he joined us, he was thinner than your son. Look at his body now!" I was uncomfortable. I blushed, but that was all I could do. A few days later I saw the young man training at the facility.

He came to the gym regularly, and I did indeed notice an improvement in his physique. He was getting stronger and building up good muscle tone. Whenever the trainer was not available, he used to come to me to ask for some advice or to show him how to operate a piece of equipment.

The sales ploy in Zaccot's office continued with other potential members. The demonstrations of my physical fitness, although sporadic, irritated me. I felt uncomfortable standing in front of strangers while Monsieur Zaccot, his arm draped around my shoulder, claimed that only a few months earlier I had been fatter, slimmer, or weaker, depending on the condition of the person he was trying to persuade. Many times I thought of leaving the place, but I was so motivated to continue my workouts that I never could.

Every year the Zaccot fitness center organized an event to promote its benefits to the affluent of Cairo. The event ended with the fittest members of the center competing at bodybuilding, bench-pressing, weight lifting, and push-ups. It usually was held at a large, posh facility, and drinks and food were served. I agreed to participate in one of these competitions because I wanted to invite my father and his friends. I knew he would enjoy the food, the drinks, and, above all, showing off his son to his friends.

On the night of the event I joined about eleven other guys in the locker room at the facility where the event was being held. We had to wear swim trunks and cover our bodies with an oily, silvery solution to get a better effect when the lights were projected on us.

I was barely ahead of my closest competitor after the bodybuilding demonstrations and the push-up contest. That meant the overall winner would be determined by the bench-press contest. My opponent was from a wealthy Lebanese family. On many occasions we trained together at the center, motivating each other. We had a good relationship. I was confident I was going to take first place. I knew from our training sessions that I could bench-press much more weight than he could.

Monsieur Zaccot came up to the podium, picked up the microphone, and announced in a dramatic tone that the bench press, the last and decisive competition, was about to start. The weights increased progressively for each of us. Suspense was building, and the audience applauded wildly as we continued to bench-press ever-heavier weights. We both knew the final two sets were crucial.

An officiating trainer lifted each weight bar and placed it in our extended hands. My opponent went first and managed to lift it with significant difficulty. I felt confident I would do better. But in each of the previous rounds, the trainer had asked if we were ready before he placed the bar in our hands. He followed this protocol during the previous round with my opponent. But while I was still readying myself, he dropped the bar on me with no warning. I managed to avoid a serious accident by controlling its fall and stopping it with my hands and chest. My opponent won first place.

I stayed calm. I knew I deserved to win and that the trainer had deliberately thrown the contest so that the wealthy competitor won. That was when I decided I was finished with Monsieur Zaccot's fitness center. The audience did not notice what had happened. Most people thought that I simply could not lift the weight.

I returned to the locker room, took a long, hot shower, and joined Dad and his friends at their table. They were having a good time. As soon as he saw me, my father stood up and proclaimed proudly in his loud voice that I was his son. He embraced me and said in Greek, "You know, Jacobimou ["my Jacob" in Greek], I don't care how they selected the winner: for me and my friends you are the best among them." In front of everyone present, to my embarrassment, he put his hand on my head and gave me his blessing in Greek and in Hebrew. He kissed me on both cheeks and whispered in my ear, *Ayin takhassou; mati na mi se piassi* ("May the evil eye go on your butt, and may the evil eye never catch you"), an expression he frequently used.

Many young people came to our table to talk to me and show their friends that they knew me. When I noticed that Monsieur Zaccot did not seem to be especially busy at his table, I went to him and asked if he would grant me a couple of minutes. When we were alone, I stared firmly at him and said, "Monsieur Zaccot, I'm not coming to your center anymore." Surprised and upset, he asked repeatedly, "But why? Why?" I judged his reaction to be sincere. I replied, "Because what I am doing in your fitness center, supporting your false statements, is not right. And what your trainer did to me tonight was disgusting and unfair." I turned my back and left. I was certain he figured I was being impulsive and that I would show up as usual at the center the following week. To him it would be stupid for such a poor young man to reject membership in his fancy club.

I returned to my father's table satisfied with my actions. I watched him and his friends joking, eating, drinking, and having fun as though they were teenagers. That was the best reward I could ever earn. Dad and I took the streetcar home together late that night. When we got off at the terminal, which was within walking distance of our house, we sat on a bench, and I looked at the shining stars, took a deep breath, and squeezed my father's hand. He broke the silence by saying, "I was very proud watching you during the competition in the presence of my friends." We enjoyed a long silence again, holding hands and looking at the sky. Then suddenly he stood up and said, "Let's go to sleep. It's not good for an athlete like you to stay up so late."

* * *

I did not get involved in politics in general. But Israel was constantly on my mind. A Zionist group approached me when I was in my late teens. They needed a place to meet. Their leader wanted to come to my house with a few of his colleagues. He explained that, in order to avoid attracting attention, they had to periodically change the places in which they met. He said I did not have to worry about any repercussions because they would carry prayer books. "If the police come in, we'll open the books and start praying; it works every time," he assured me. I thought, *If it works every time, the police are aware of your activities, and the meeting at my house might be when you'll get caught.* It was not reassuring at all. He did not appear to be well organized and did not provide the reason for the meetings.

For me the risks were a good deal greater than any potential benefit. I was convinced that Jews had the right to have their own nation; I did not need to be lectured on the subject. In my view the only way I could help was to go to Israel and fight with the Jewish soldiers. And this was not possible because I could not afford to go, and my focus was on my studies.

My relatives seemed resigned and even happy with their positions in life. Although they tried to improve their situations as much as possible, they knew all too well that they could go only so far. I would hear them say that they had to play the cards they had been dealt. They claimed that, in Egypt, you can never rise above the social caste to which you were born.

I did not agree. I wanted to break the mold and be the first in our family to get to a higher caste. I wanted to change the destiny of our family and future generations. I did not want any of our relatives to go to bed at night without food, as I did when we lived in Alexandria. For me, my studies were the only means I had to reach my dreams. I could not let the environment and conditions that surrounded me decide my destiny. I dreamed of becoming a doctor.

CHAPTER 3

BY THE END of World War II, Egypt had become the general headquarters for the British in the Middle East. But at the time, Britain was being pressured to pull its forces out of Palestine and India, and the Egyptian people also wanted the British to accelerate their departure from Egypt. In early 1946 Egyptians brutally demonstrated their anger by means of escalating attacks on British and European properties.

Hatred toward foreigners in general and Jews in particular surfaced with alarming intensity. Almost every Friday evening and Saturday morning, Jews on their way to the synagogues in Daher were attacked by young Arab men armed with sticks covered with nails. The fanatics suffered no legal consequences for their actions, as they had the tacit approval of the police. The Jewish victims had no rights; their complaints were fruitless. The vigilante groups would openly beat Jews in the streets, even in the busiest areas of downtown Cairo.

One afternoon as I was leaving school, three classmates told me that a group of Arabs had beaten them repeatedly during the previous few days. This group always attacked my classmates at a certain streetcar-line intersection. As soon as my friends passed by, swarms of Arab men would surge from coffee shops and jump off speeding streetcars with their sticks covered in nails. "They beat us and hurt us," one of my classmates said. "Last time they carried knives, and one day they even might kill us! Can you please come with us and help us?" Although they lived far from my home, I could not refuse such a desperate plea.

That day, as soon as we approached the square where they had been attacked, I could feel my classmates becoming more anxious. Suddenly a group of Arab men ran toward us, soon joined by another group. Some were adults wearing beards and turbans. They surrounded us and started yelling at us and pushing us. Many of them waved their nail-covered sticks and knives toward us.

We were younger and smaller, and there were fewer of us, and obviously we wanted to avoid a fight. I tried to appease the one who seemed to be the Arabs' leader and explained to him that we were students just trying to get home. The group was swelling as more men appeared, seemingly out of nowhere. Their voices were getting louder as they yelled, *Yahoudi*; *Sahyouni* ("Jew; Zionist"). They grabbed my shirt and my neck, and their hands covered my face. As we became surrounded by an increasingly large and violent mob, I realized we were in grave danger. I yelled to my friends in French, "Run with all your might!"

To open a path through the densely packed aggressors, I started throwing punches as hard and as fast as I could.

Their faces bloodied, some of our assailants began to fall on each other. They did not anticipate such a response from a usually passive group. In their moment of surprise we broke free and ran like mad. We dispersed; two classmates took a streetcar away from the scene, and I ended up at the house of a third classmate, Hamawi. We managed to escape the notice of the mob by using a back door.

His parents were not home, so we told his older sister what had happened. She offered us a cold drink and towels so we could wash our faces. She then went to the window and peeked through the shades. "There is a large mob running through the streets trying to find you." She came back and sat down with us. "Stay here," she said. "It's Friday night. Our parents will be here soon; you can join us for the Shabbat dinner, and then you can go home or even sleep here with us. We won't have you getting hurt." She was grateful that I had brought her brother home unharmed. I said I could not accept her invitation; my parents were certain to be worried because I was so late. I would stay a bit longer, until the mob dispersed, and then leave.

After a while I looked through the window again. With the area dark and quiet, I figured it was safe to leave. "May God protect you. Be careful," the sister whispered. The square had emptied, and I took a streetcar home. When I got there, Dad was waiting for me in the living room. I explained my lateness with an excuse about an unanticipated sports event. He was glad to see me and did not press me with questions.

The next afternoon I went out to tend to my Saturday errands. Afterward, when I walked back into our apartment, I stopped at the door. Dad, Tante Marie, and an Egyptian man were sitting in the living room. I sensed that the man was important because a plate of sweets and an assortment of coffee cups were on the coffee table, an honor that Tante Marie would bestow only upon important guests.

"Ah, here he is," said the Egyptian man. "You are Jacob." He looked me up and down. "I was just telling your parents that in our police headquarters, rumors abound that you were almost killed." He then repeated what he had told my parents, explaining that he was with the secret police. "Will you please join us?" He was pointing to a chair in front of him. It was more an order than a request. He was sitting on the couch between my father and Tante Marie, and I suspected he probably wanted to watch my face while talking to me.

He said, "Let me save you some time and tell you what we know about you." As he described my life, I was completely shocked. He knew I was attending l'École Cattaui, that I had led the school strike, that we had won a basketball championship, and that I practiced at the Maccabi Daher Club. He then paused to gauge the impact of his statements.

Up to that point, he had spoken with a slight smile and a soft voice. Suddenly, though, his face became serious and his voice louder. Leaning toward me, he demanded, "Now that you are aware of just how much we know about you, tell me which Zionist group you belong to."

I looked him straight in the eye and told him in a calm and firm voice that I did not belong to any political group. I ended by asserting, "Officer, believe me, you who know so much about me should have also discovered that I care only about my studies and sports."

During the interrogation Dad and Tante Marie kept silent but wore their anxiety on their faces. Tante Marie poured some fresh coffee in the officer's cup, and Dad presented him with the plate of cookies. The officer took a sip of coffee, cleaned his mustache with a handkerchief, looked deep into my eyes, and said, "Yes. I believe you; I just wanted to make sure." Then he added with some arrogance, "I can tell you were not lying; if you had been, I would have taken you directly to the police station, where I'm certain you would have told us everything." His loud, sadistic laugh resonated throughout the house. Then he put his left arm around my father's shoulder and his right hand on Tante Marie's knee. The liberties he took through intimidation filled me with outrage. "But you don't have to worry. You're clean," he jeered, releasing his grip.

Pointing his finger at me, he said, "You know, one of the leaders of the group who keeps attacking your classmates is a sports fanatic, just like you." He mentioned the young man's name and told me that he lived not far from our school. Finally the intelligence officer stood up to leave, and as my father held the door open, the officer said to me, "I know this young man well, and I think you two would get along. I will talk to him. I'll give him your name and ask him to find you."

After he left, I had the difficult task of explaining to Dad and Tante Marie what had happened the previous evening. Disturbed by these details, Tante Marie whispered to my father, "He could have been killed."

"Yes, but thank God he is alive and in good health," my father responded. I could sense some pride in his voice.

Then curiosity took over, and he asked, "How come you did not even get a scratch?"

"I did not give them the chance to touch me," I answered. Hearing this, my father beamed from ear to ear.

The following Monday I took my customary route to school but stayed alert lest the assailants seek revenge. As I approached Sakakini Square, I started feeling more secure. But then a bulky young Arab man jumped out of a moving streetcar and headed directly toward me. I feared that many more would follow him, but he was alone. "Are you Jacob?" he asked. I looked him over; he was well dressed and smiling.

"Yes," I answered and, fearing a fight might break out, put down my bag.

He began, "I saw the officer who came to your house on Saturday evening; he gave me your name and said good things about you." I was silent; I did not know what to say. I was a Jew who had a fight with a gang of Arab men. Why would the officer speak well of me?

The young man went on. "The officer told me that you are a good athlete and that you play basketball." I nodded and said we had a basketball team at l'École Cattaui. He took me by the arm, I picked up my bag, and we began walking toward my school. After a few steps he stopped and said, "From now on, our gang will no longer bother you or your classmates. I swear on Allah almighty that I'll keep my promise. If those men bother you, just give them my name and tell them that you are my friend." I thanked him and said I appreciated his help very much. When we arrived at my school, he added, "We, too, have a basketball team. Can we organize a game with your school?"

I said, "Yes, of course. Just let me know when—" He stopped me in midsentence and said, "We'll schedule it next time we meet." He hurried back to catch a streetcar.

To this day I am puzzled by the extraordinary behavior of the secret police officer and the leader of the gang. At a time when patriotism meant persecuting foreigners, especially Jews, we could not have been luckier. The leader of the gang did contact me again, and we got our teams together for a basketball game—we played for fun, mixing players from both teams, and did not keep score.

Our studies went on with no further disturbances. We were the pioneer students of our high school, as planned. Each time we were promoted to the next grade, l'École Cattaui had to squeeze more students into the building. After our second year, the entire high school was transferred to the more spacious Jewish Community School in Abbassieh, also known as l'École Sybile.

The school in Abbassieh was about a twenty-minute walk from Cattaui, and this new location offered us more space and better facilities. The modern auditorium, which had a large screen, many blackboards, and comfortable amphitheater seating, impressed us all. We had never seen an auditorium before, much less sat in one. We had excellent sports facilities with modern equipment, far better than what we had at Cattaui. The high school classrooms were built on the roof terrace, where we also spent our breaks. Because we were at the top of the building, we could not play with balls, but we did not mind so much since we considered ourselves to be mature students and spent our free time talking, eating, and reading. We waited until school ended to go downstairs to use the basketball courts and track as well as the gymnastic and fitness equipment.

* * *

"Have you heard the news?" Tante Marie asked one day as soon as I came home from school. She could hardly wait to tell me but still wanted to pique my curiosity.

"By the look on your face, it must be some good news; tell me what's going on," I replied.

She smiled. "Your sister is engaged."

"Oh, wonderful," I said. "And who is the—"

"Wait—that's not all," she said, interrupting me. "Léon is also engaged." I could easily guess what had happened.

My sister, Denise, in 1947

Léon and Denise had many friends in common, most of whom they had met at parties and clubs. Denise and Léon had been going out more and more frequently with Victor Abada and Victor's sister Aimée. They had come to our house many times.

I said, "Tante, I think I know what's going on: Denise with Victor and Léon with Aimée—an exchange of brothers and sisters."

"Yes," she said. "Isn't it wonderful?"

Victor, who had worked with Léon at Agami and Banque Belge, was a tall, handsome young man; without his heavy eyeglasses he looked a bit like the actor Victor Mature. Victor was eleven years older than Denise, who turned eighteen that year. Victor's sister Aimée had full lips, big black eyes, dark skin, and a beautiful body. She was a year younger than Léon, who was then twenty-two.

Victor and Aimée's parents, Menasha and Camille Abada, had been born in Iraq, and both had come to Egypt at a young age. They had five children, all born in Cairo—three boys and two girls. Victor was the oldest, and Aimée was the third child. But after the engagement, disagreements quickly surfaced between the two families. Madame Abada, Léon's and Denise's soon-to-be mother-in-law, was a strong-willed woman who insisted that both weddings be handled her way. Her demands, of course, did not sit well with my explosive father. He disliked her, and the schedule for the weddings became a major issue. Madame Abada insisted that both couples marry on the same afternoon. She wanted Léon and Aimée's wedding to be held one hour before Denise and Victor's. Denise and Léon implored Dad to accede to Madame Abada's demands. He finally gave in.

On the day of the weddings, in June of 1947, I donned a suit and tie and went to the synagogue. I was not aware that Denise was alone in our home. Everyone in our family had to be present for Léon's wedding and did not realize that, as a young bride, Denise needed help getting dressed. Fortunately my teacher and high school principal, Youssef Salama, a Karaite Jew, had recently married and had rented an apartment just in front of ours. His wife offered to help and even lent Denise her wedding dress and bridal accessories. On the day of the wedding, however, Mrs. Salama had to take care of her newborn baby. Denise dressed by herself, then stepped out on the balcony for Mrs. Salama's approval. Many other neighbors also chatted from the balconies and windows, and when they saw her, they clapped and made the traditional joyous Middle Eastern sound called *zaghlat* in Arabic.

Mrs. Salama came to the balcony and told Denise in a soft, sweet voice, *Enti aroussa gamila awi awi, enti zey el amar* ("You are a very, very beautiful bride; you are like the moon"). This encouraging comment gave the young bride confidence. To this day Denise has fond memories of Mrs. Salama.

* * *

The owner of our building was an old woman, Mademoiselle Emilie, who had no relatives. Each time we went up or down the stairs, she opened her door's little window to greet us. During our holidays we brought her a tray filled with our traditional pastries, and she did the same during hers; she was a religious member of the Syrian Orthodox Church.

Mademoiselle Emilie's health was frail. She was hospitalized for a short time, and soon afterward she died. Because she had no heirs, she had named the Syrian Orthodox Church as the sole recipient of her assets, which included the building where we lived. Her apartment remained empty for a while, but eventually the Hawaras, a woman and her three adult sons, moved in. The church offered the family free rent temporarily, until the sons could find work.

From the beginning, we sensed that the Hawaras were not friendly people. Soon after they moved in, Tante Marie knocked on their door with a tray of pastries to welcome them. The door remained closed, even though she could hear breathing behind the door. This happened every time one of us went up or down the stairs. The situation then took a turn for the worse.

Before daybreak one day a loud noise shook our bedroom floor. It lasted a few minutes, then started again in a different room. Thinking it was an earthquake, we all jumped out of our beds. When the noise and shaking persisted, we realized it was coming from the Hawaras, whose apartment was beneath ours.

My father opened the door to check whether something was wrong on the Hawaras' floor. An anonymous note lay at our doorstep. In barely legible Arabic the note informed us that we would face more problems because, as Jews, we did not have the right to make noise by walking into our home at night.

The note's focus on our religion deeply worried Dad and Tante Marie. Throughout the time we had lived in the midst of Muslim neighbors, we had maintained a good and friendly relationship with them. The Hawaras, however, did not stop harassing us. We continued to get the same noise treatment regularly at around two or three o'clock in the morning.

The three jobless sons slept during the day, while we were busy with our studies and work, and stayed awake at night, when they set about to prevent us from sleeping. Each son would knock on the ceiling with a stick to shake our floor and our beds. Their relentless obsession started to affect our lives. We were all on edge; the sleep deprivation grew unbearable. Tante Marie, trying to appease us, said she would talk to Mrs. Hawara.

"Women can always settle problems better than men," she claimed. She went to their floor and knocked on their door many times at various hours, but the person breathing behind the door never answered.

The torture the Hawaras inflicted on us took its toll. We grew irritable and argumentative for no reason. We felt frustrated because we did not have an effective way to stop them. We did not think it would help to file a complaint with the police, because we worried about retaliation against Jews. We went to the Syrian Orthodox Church, and a clerk took note of our complaint. After many calls a supervisor told us that the church did not get involved in issues among neighbors. It was a desperate situation; sometimes we did not sleep the whole night, just anticipating the knocks and the shaking. But the end of this nightmare came about unexpectedly.

A grocery store was located on our street. It was a modest outlet, convenient for us and our neighbors. We could call the owner, Haj Abdou, from the balcony and tell him what we needed. He then placed our items in a basket. The basket was attached to a rope that ran to the street from our balcony so we could pull up the items we had ordered. We even had a line of credit with him and settled it every weekend. He was a religious, peaceful, and kind man, a widower who lived with his two big, strong adult sons.

At one point Haj Abdou was absent from his store for a long time. When we asked his sons about him, they said he had been arrested for allegedly belonging to the Ikhwan El Mouslimoun, the Muslim Brotherhood, which the Egyptian government considered to be a terrorist group. While in prison, Haj Abdou was tortured and endured long hours of interrogation, but he was released after the police could find no good reason to keep him. When he returned, I immediately went to his store to greet him. He was pale and had lost a lot of weight. I inquired about his health and told him we had missed him. He explained that an investigator had said that the Hawaras had sent a letter to the police accusing him of belonging to the Muslim Brotherhood. I shared with him our troubles and our frustration at not being able to stop them.

He embraced me and whispered in my ear, "Don't worry, my friend; my sons will take care of them."

When I returned to the neighborhood late that evening, Haj Abdou's sons were sitting on chairs at the door to our building. They were holding large clubs.

"Our father was kept in prison for no reason because of them. We will keep them imprisoned in their home for a *good* reason," said one brother.

"Unless they choose to deal with this," the other brother added, waving his thick club. Their surveillance lasted a few days. Haj Abdou's sons took shifts guarding the door to our building day and night. The Hawaras could not get out of their home.

Finally the mother came down one day, kneeled in front of Haj Abdou and his sons, and cried, "We are starving; we have to buy food; please let us out." She told Haj Abdou she was sorry for what her sons had done to him. They did it without her knowledge. She said her sons were good-for-nothing bums. They never worked; she had to ask for charity from the church to feed her family. She also said the church had given them the apartment rent-free only for a certain period, until her sons could find a job. Since her sons were unwilling to work, the church was evicting them at the end of the month. She begged Haj Abdou and his sons to allow her to go and promised that her sons would no longer bother anyone.

The knocks on our bedroom floors stopped the same night. A few days later the Hawaras quietly left our building.

Bon débarras ("good riddance"), Tante Marie declared in French with a sigh of relief.

* * *

My father assembled us for a special Saturday night dinner some months after Léon's and Denise's weddings. That night, we waited for him to return from the synagogue. As he stepped into the house, he offered his Greek and Hebrew good wishes in his typical loud voice: *Kali evthomatha; Shabouwah tov* ("Have a good week").

Gomhetna hadra ("May we have a green week"), Tante Marie replied in Arabic. The color green was supposed to bring good luck and happiness. Having Denise and her husband, Victor, together with Aimée and Léon for dinner was an exceptional event, because the couples did not get along.

Soon after their weddings their relationships had soured. Disagreements and fights set in, exacerbated by the parents-in-law on both sides. They expected their sons, Victor and Léon, to defend their daughters and remain more loyal to blood kin than to married kin. If Léon had a fight with Aimée, her parents forced her brother Victor to avenge her by picking a fight with Denise. My father would do the same, expecting Léon to pick a fight with Aimée in defense of Denise.

This craziness produced a regular vicious circle, with constant arguments among the two couples and their respective parents-in-law. To bring them together at our house was remarkable. My father must have used all his salesmanship to persuade them to join us. He cooked his specialty, arnaki may youvetsi—lamb with orzo. He prepared the lamb with a special marinade, the ingredients of which he kept secret, even from Tante Marie. We knew that he used oregano, wine, and olive leaves, but that was about as much as we could find out.

After we were all seated at the dinner table, Dad passed around some strong, aromatic green leaves from an herb called *marsim* in Egypt (also known as rue, or herb of grace). We rubbed them on our hands and then smelled them as a good omen for a lucky and joyous "green week." He then opened a bottle of kokinelli, his favorite Greek red wine. He filled our glasses and raised his own to recite the kiddush, the blessing of the wine. We had a nice dinner; no one fought, and good humor prevailed.

After dinner my father asked us to stay at the table; he needed to talk with us. "Things are going to get tough for us Jews here in Egypt," he said. "The Palestine issue grows worse daily. A war between the Arabs and the Jews will certainly erupt when the British leave Palestine. England is not on our side—and that is not good for us." After his lengthy statement he paused, then tearfully continued, "Please, no more fights among our families; we have more serious problems to worry about. Please take good care of yourselves."

He then stood up and, with the majestic gesture of a high priest, raised his hands above our heads and recited the Jewish blessing: "May God bless you and watch upon you; may God shine his face upon you and protect you; may God be favorably disposed toward you; and may God grant you peace." He gave a special emphasis to *shalom*, the last word in the Hebrew blessing. Long after everyone had left the table and adjourned to the living room, I stayed in my chair and meditated on my father's comments. I knew he was right. We were headed toward a war in Palestine, and peace did not seem a realistic expectation. *Shalom* in Hebrew and *salam* in Arabic both mean "peace" and are used by Jews and Muslims alike in their daily greetings and prayers. I thought, *Here are two religions that use "peace" in their everyday prayers and greetings and are about to kill each other.*

* * *

The Arab-Israeli conflict and the sudden abandonment of British interests in Palestine in May of 1948 became the subject of fiery anti-Jewish speeches in the Arab countries, led by Egypt. At seventeen, I was torn between my emotional impulse to flee to Palestine and play some kind of heroic role in the creation of Israel and a more realistic and mature plan to stay in Egypt and pursue my dream of becoming a doctor. I avoided discussing this matter even with classmates and friends. My feelings and my thoughts were mine only; I was unwilling to share them.

In school one day, instead of giving his usual history lecture, our teacher of Arabic wanted us to engage in an open debate. He then asked us to suggest an interesting subject to discuss, but none of the topics we presented pleased him. He had his mind set on one topic: the Arab-Israeli conflict. He was in his late thirties, and he had excellent teaching skills; our class made substantial progress in Arabic under his tutelage. We had fun learning, and he enjoyed teaching us. He had dark circles under his eyes, and he would carry a cup of black tea to sip while giving his lessons. He also chewed something that we suspected was hashish.

Our teacher made a special effort to appear to us as a modern, open-minded Muslim. In many ways he differed from the Arabic teachers we had previously. He was more skillful and possessed a wider knowledge of world events. He made his courses more interesting by adding humor to his teaching. His idea to debate the Arab-Israeli situation, however, was not reasonable.

My classmates, though, grew excited and jumped at the chance, confident in their knowledge of Palestinian history and their debating skills. They welcomed the challenge; they were well prepared.

The discussion began in a light tone with some humor and jokes; then it escalated rapidly to a discussion of who lived in Palestine first and who had the right to the land. Soon the discussion heated up, and it became obvious that our teacher was on the losing end of the debate. I asked my zealous classmates to stop, but to no avail. They were savoring their victory. At a loss, our teacher suddenly grabbed a student who had stood up during the debate and started hitting him frantically with both hands, one stroke after the other, like a madman. He was furious. Initially the whole class was caught by surprise and remained hypnotized by our teacher's enraged reaction. We soon recovered our senses.

I held our teacher back and tried to calm him down while another student ran to find our principal.

I remember saying to the teachers and the principal who gathered in our classroom, "It's not enough for us to be beaten in the streets; now we are beaten in our own school!"

The principal fired the teacher on the spot.

* * *

Although listening to foreign radio stations was illegal, several classmates received current news about events in Palestine through the BBC, and we all rejoiced when, on May 14, 1948, in accordance with the 1947 UN Partition Plan, the Jewish Agency for Israel, led by David Ben-Gurion, declared the successful creation of the state of Israel. The members of the Arab League immediately declared war against the new nation.

During these volatile times we had to pass our Egyptian baccalaureate exams, which were held over the course of several days at Fouad I University. Given throughout Egypt on the same date, they were prepared and supervised by the Egyptian board of education. Students from our school were easily identified as being of foreign descent and a different religion. We felt nervous and scared. We had to take our most important exams in hostile territory.

Still, I completed all the exams with ease. I experienced difficulty only during the Arabic-language test. Our written exam required us to write about the death of the Arab nationalist hero Abd al-Qadir al-Husseini, who led the so-called Army of the Holy War. It took me a long time to overcome my abhorrence of writing about a man who had promised the annihilation of the Jewish population. I had to, or I would fail my most important final exam. Mentally, I simply replaced every mention of his name with that of an Israeli hero.

A few weeks later we received the results of our exams. Our class did well. I received honors in French and math and ranked within the top 10 percent nationwide. My grades qualified me to pursue my studies tuition-free at an Egyptian university. However, this was not to be. Just after I received my exam results, my father had a heart attack, which was caused by his clogged arteries, and it traumatized our whole family. For several weeks, his life was in danger. It took him a long time to recover, and we all thought that he would not be able to resume his work.

Because of the country's political situation it was not safe for me to attend an Egyptian university, and with my father's illness, long-term plans were not realistic. On the day I should have been celebrating my good grades, I felt depressed. My dream to become a doctor had been shattered. Moving up the social ladder seemed impossible. I remained apathetic for weeks. I was eighteen and had to find a job and pursue a life of routine and resignation, like the rest of my family and many of my friends. There seemed to be no way out. Everyone in our family expected me to look for work, but I procrastinated. I knew that finding a menial job was unavoidable, but I simply was not ready.

The Maccabi Daher Club had ceased its activities for security reasons. Nevertheless I continued playing basketball at school with some of my old classmates and at the YMCA. I intensified my reading, grabbing any book I could find. I also played poker with a group of scoundrels—a bad decision, I soon found out. My opponents, smelling blood, realized that I did not have enough money to call their bluffs. I not only lost my weekly allowance but also had to borrow money to cover my losses.

My brothers and sister did not notice my emotional state; they were busy with their own problems. I did not, however, escape my father's scrutiny. He sensed my frustration, but he was wise enough to understand that I needed to be left alone. In our family it was unusual not to get involved in one another's business. In my case Dad acted as if everything was all right. He waited for my mood to change before he encouraged me to find a job.

* * *

Denise announced one evening that one of her friends knew of a job opening for an assistant sales clerk. She thought that it was a good opportunity for me. The next morning I borrowed a suit and tie from my brother Saby. The suit was too big for me and quite uncomfortable. But as my family was pressing me to find a job, I had to show that I was trying.

Denise took me to the store and introduced me to her friend, who presented me to her boss. I was then instructed to stand by the door and invite pedestrians in to take advantage of the wonderful offerings. I tried to do as I was told, but when someone came in, I did not know what to say. With no coaching, I was a total failure.

Denise stopped by late that evening. Her friend pulled her to the side. I saw them both waving their arms in a hopeless manner. I did not make it. My job lasted one day. Denise took me back home without a word. She was disappointed. I had only one thought in mind: to get out of my ridiculously large suit and the suffocating tie that had annoyed me the whole day.

Now that I had tried to find work, my father felt emboldened to search on my behalf, too. He asked me to go to a printing shop that was within walking distance of our house. The Jewish owner ran his business with his daughter and brother. The daughter, in charge of finance, prepared a math test for me, which I passed easily, and they hired me the same day.

My job—to keep track of the inventory and the accounting in the warehouse—was simple; it did not require mathematical skills. After a few weeks I grew bored, so I found a way to kill time. We had an Arab employee who helped us carry the large, heavy rolls of printing paper; he was a weight lifter. We found an iron bar to which we attached the paper rolls and challenged each other in weight lifting when we had nothing else to do. Then we began challenging each other in wrestling. These friendly bouts allowed us to have fun in an otherwise boring environment. The owner caught us one day in the middle of a wrestling session. He summoned us to his office. As soon as I went in, I told him that I was the one to blame and would take full responsibility for what had happened. He fired me, but I was glad that my

Arab coworker was spared. When the owner's daughter handed me my pay, she said her father had already been planning to let me go because I was not the kind of employee he wanted.

"He prefers the fireball kind, not the thinker type, like you." I did not say a word; I took the money and left. This was another job I did not mind losing.

* * *

The doorbell rang late one evening. My father and Tante Marie were sleeping, so I hastened to open the door. As he tried to catch his breath, one of Léon's friends asked me to awaken my father because it was important. Dad and Tante Marie came out of their bedroom, looking pale and scared. We all listened anxiously.

"First of all, I want to reassure you; there is no serious accident or death."

"For God's sake, tell us what's going on," Dad yelled.

Léon and his wife, Aimée, had been arrested at the Mutuelle des Employés de Banques, the club where they spent time with friends. The Egyptian police had raided it, closed the doors, and allowed no one to leave. After a long time they took all the Jews in the group to the police station. Before he left our house, the man promised to let us know as soon as he got more news. We did not sleep all night. My father prayed, and Tante Marie cried. I tried to read, but I could not concentrate.

The next day we learned that Léon and the other men had been taken to a police station and imprisoned. Aimée and the other women were taken to a different police station and also jailed. Secret police officers kept them for four days under heavy interrogation. The investigators wanted to know if any Zionist activities took place at the club.

Then, not long afterward, Denise got a scare. She noticed someone watching and following her as she pushed her newborn baby, Camille, in the stroller to the market and on other errands. Denise did not pay much attention until she received a notice to present herself at the police station with her birth and marriage certificates, school records, and rent, electricity, and other bills. The police wanted to make sure that she could prove her identity.

When she arrived at the police station, the officer in charge spent a long time analyzing the documents. When he was convinced of her identity, the officer told her, "You know, we received an anonymous letter a few months ago accusing you of being an Israeli spy. We have to check all these letters; we never know." Then, before she left, he smiled and told her, "You have a nice little baby girl. She is the reason we did not arrest you. Go in peace." Denise believed that one of the Hawaras had sent the anonymous letter.

* * *

Israel's victory in the Arab-Israeli War had a devastating effect on King Farouk and his government, which still depended on British support to stay in power. The Egyptian government declared martial law and polarized Egyptian politics into pro-British and anti-British positions. This situation increased the influence of the military, fundamentalist Muslims, and particularly the extremist Muslim Brotherhood.

Under these circumstances we tried to maintain our normal life and daily routine. The hostile environment, however, affected us emotionally. We were the only Jews in our neighborhood, so we tried to keep a low profile. When walking on our narrow street, I lowered my head, slumped my shoulders, and avoided people who stood in front of their stores or in the middle of the street. I did not engage in conversation with them, as I had in the past.

Because we had good relationships with our neighbors, and because our family always treated them with respect and care, they spared us any aggressive physical or verbal abuse. We were not, however, spared the aggressiveness and hostility outside our neighborhood. And I am certain our neighbors exhibited their hatred for Jews and foreigners in other areas of the city.

In the last months of 1948, however, Saby, a young man of few words, suddenly grew interested in everything and everyone around him. He whistled and hummed songs in the bathroom, in our bedroom, and even on the balcony, where he spent long hours before going to sleep. Saby was in love. He was twenty-two, and she was seventeen. Juliette Gelardine was a member of a Sephardic family originally from Turkey.

Saby and Juliette met when they were working at Maison Cicurel, she as a salesperson in the perfume section and he as a sales clerk in the fabric and women's apparel sections. They fell in love and wanted to marry.

They had a short engagement, because Saby had been laid off. Sales at the Jewish-owned Maison Cicurel had dropped because of the boycott of Jewish businesses after Israel was created and because of a deteriorating economy.

The layoff's effect on their meager budget devastated Juliette and Saby. Their only option was to immigrate to Israel.

They were married in March of 1949 with little fanfare, and they left soon thereafter. More than seven hundred thousand Jews immigrated to Israel from all over the world during this period, almost doubling its population. This massive relocation created a heavy burden for the new nation. When Saby and Juliette arrived in Israel, they had to live in temporary camps and tents until they could learn the language and find jobs. Conditions in Israel at that time, known as the austerity period, proved extremely rough.

* * *

The year 1949 emerged as one of the toughest years of my own life as well. That was the year after I left school with my useless baccalaureate diploma and held a couple of insignificant jobs at which I failed miserably. I had no idea what I would do with my life, and I did not really care. I was a drifter with no purpose.

One day, during a basketball scrimmage at the YMCA, I almost fainted under the scorching sun. I was dizzy, disoriented, and experiencing painful cramps. I barely made it home. After several exams the doctor concluded that I had scarlet fever, which kept me home for several weeks. Soon after that I came home shivering with another high fever. My father called the doctor to our home, and the diagnosis crashed on us like thunder—I had typhoid fever.

The doctor told my father and Tante Marie that this serious and highly contagious disease would prove fatal if I had a relapse; the fever had to stop within the next two weeks. I glanced at my father and saw that his face was ashen. Tante Marie could not hold back her tears. I was delirious during the next few nights, and then I started feeling better.

Every morning my father came to my bedside and prayed, imploring God to save my life. I heard him repeat my name for a long time: "Jacobimou, Jacobimou." A few weeks later, I felt strong enough to leave the house for the first time.

But the next day I had difficulty urinating, and after a few days, my urine turned dark brown. I lived with that condition for several months, consulting all the doctors my father knew. I went through several medical exams, but no one identified my mysterious condition. Some suggested that it might have resulted from a lack of vitamins; illnesses such as beriberi and scurvy were among the diseases mentioned, most of which I did not recognize or bother to understand.

My father and Tante Marie were at a loss about what to do. They were suffering, I'm sure, even more than I was. Finally Tante Marie came to me and my father with an idea: "I think I should take Jacob to the shrine of Rabbi Moshe ben Maimon," she said to him. My father enthusiastically agreed. "You must have caught the evil eye," he said to me, "and Rabbi ben Maimon can rid you of it."

Rabbi Moshe ben Maimon, also known as Maimonides, was born in Cordoba, Spain, in 1135. He lived for around forty years in Egypt, where he practiced medicine and served as a rabbi. People believed he performed miracles, saving the lives of poor people and notorious personalities alike. After his death, in 1204, his tomb in Cairo became a shrine where the desperate sought cures.

There was no way I could avoid being part of Tante Marie's plan, so a few days later, she and I headed to Haret

El Yahoud, the Jewish quarter. We walked the narrow streets and entered a small and decrepit old building. Tante Marie knew her way around and performed all the rituals required. We then followed an old man who led us to a small room with a low ceiling and two narrow couches that served as beds.

Tante Marie whispered, "We have to lie down, make our wishes, and sleep. If the rabbi appears in our dreams, it means that he has heard our requests, and our wishes will come true." After I lay down, she said, "Try to summon him in your dreams; try hard."

She then lay down on the other couch. I'm sure she wanted to make a wish of her own. She was eager to have a child, but I knew no prayers could have helped her.

We spent many hours in the dark and silent room. Although I was not an ardent believer in the evil eye, or in miraculous cures, I closed my eyes to please Tante Marie and dozed off for a little while. Probably because of the environment we were in and all the rituals Tante Marie had performed, I did envision some figures wearing beards and old-style religious attire. When I became too restless to lie down, I got up off the couch.

My aunt sat up and asked me in a low, tired voice, "Did you see him? Did you see the rabbi?" I nodded. "Good," she said. "Your father will be happy."

"And you?" I asked. No, she did not; she said she could not fall asleep. I felt sorry for her.

I continued to see doctors, but none of them could give us a diagnosis. I did not fear for my life, but I was eager to know what was wrong. I occasionally felt a sharp pain in my back that forced me to lie down and caused me to break out in a cold sweat. Still, my health improved slowly, but I was not as healthy or as fit as I once was. Most of the time I stayed home and read books.

* * *

"Get dressed and come with me. I want to show you something," Dad said as he stood at my bedroom door. It was not an order but a plea, designed to coax me out of the house. I felt sorry for him; he must have suffered so much on my account, and because of his heart condition I did not want to turn down his request. We went out together, and he took me to Emad El Din Street, where he stopped in front of a store and asked me, "Hey, what do you think of this?"

"This what?" I asked.

"This department store! Can't you see it?" I took a step backward to read the name written on the building.

"Maison I. Gattegno," I replied.

"Yes. It's owned by Jews who came from Thessaloniki," he said.

I looked at him, puzzled. "So what?" I asked.

"Well, I know the Carassos; they are related to the owner, and I believe I can get you a job. I wanted to make sure that you are up to it."

I did not answer.

"I'm sure it will work out. They are nice people," my father said. It was the beginning of December in 1949, a few months since I finished school. I had spent the intervening months wandering, apathetic and ill.

A few days later my father introduced me to Jacques and Ino Carasso and to Paul Somek, Gattegno's director and chief executive officer. After a short interview they took me to an office occupied by three men. Two were busy typing. The third man was Albert Gattegno, the nephew of Silvio Gattegno, who owned the department store. There was an empty desk, which I assumed—correctly—would be mine. Jacquot Matalon, one of the typists, was in charge of that office. I found out later that he was Paul Somek's nephew. Jacquot told me that his office was responsible for all administrative work related to purchasing, including correspondence, placing orders, and securing import licenses.

He explained that my job would consist of picking up copies of the sales receipts from the cashiers and making sure that the money collected by them matched the totals on the receipts. Most important, I would keep statistics on the sales of each product. The statistics had great importance and were followed closely by the cashiers, the heads of each department, and management. He also told me that after learning my new job, I would be in charge of preparing and securing import licenses from the Egyptian authorities for the many products the company imported from Europe.

Maison Gattegno, located in a three-story building, was small compared to other department stores, such as Cicurel and Orosdi-Back, but it was just as popular. Silvio Gattegno, a short, feeble, white-haired old man, was the son of the founder, Isaac Gattegno, and did not seem to have an office. He came to the store late in the afternoon once or twice a week and had a special chair reserved for him close to the entrance. We knew when he was in the store because Mr. Somek and the Carassos would immediately leave their offices and walk downstairs to talk to him. Several family members, relatives, and friends of his also worked at the store. Not all of them had specific jobs. We never really learned what Albert Gattegno and the Carassos did, for example, but they used their offices every day. The rest of the salaried employees were mainly Jews and Italians.

My first day on the job was a disaster. I made several mistakes in recording and adding the numbers and could not reconcile the cash collected from the cashiers with the numbers I recorded on my statistics sheets. The cashiers were responsible for any missing amount; therefore they anxiously awaited my tally. I reviewed my work several times, checking all the numbers one by one, and each time I found many errors. As I erased my numerous mistakes, my spreadsheets ended up with holes that I patched with adhesive tape. I sweated as the end of the working day neared, and I constantly checked my watch. Finally the cash on hand delivered by the cashiers and the sums shown on my spreadsheets matched. With a sigh of relief I took my papers downstairs, where Paul Somek and the Carassos were waiting; they were ready to go home. I spread the sheets on a counter and showed them the numbers. The numbers were correct, but the spreadsheets looked awful. I sensed from the looks they exchanged that they were shocked by the spectacle. I went home convinced that I would be fired the following day.

Fortunately, my work quickly and noticeably improved. After a couple of months I could finish my statistics in a few hours and dedicate the rest of the day to other jobs, such as preparing import licenses and typing letters to suppliers. With time my accounting ability improved so much that I could add the sales numbers in my head, just by glancing up and down each column. Paul Somek, Jacques Carasso, and other managers often came to my office to watch my virtuosic addition. They would sometimes challenge our accountants to beat me with an adding machine. I became a popular person at Gattegno.

One day, after I was on the job for a few months, Jacquot Matalon mentioned that he was leaving early because he had basketball practice that evening. He explained that the Egyptian Basketball Federation organized two basketball tournaments every year for corporate teams. One tournament allowed the participation on each team of two players from the federation's first division—the one with the most experienced and skillful players. The other tournament did not allow any first-division players to participate.

"At Gattegno we have two teams that participate in both tournaments. We do not perform so badly with the first team, but we get creamed every year with our second team. You see," he explained, "on the first team, we have the Behar brothers, Zaki and Bertie; they are both experienced players who also play with the Maccabi first-division club. Since they cannot play in the second tournament, we lose almost every game."

I had seen Zaki Behar play in the past, and I had thought I recognized him downstairs on Gattegno's ground floor. He was in charge of deliveries and transportation. As I recalled from watching him play with Maccabi, he was short, energetic, and a good ball handler. I did not know Bertie Behar. Jacquot then asked me if I had ever played the game; I said that I had played at school but that I had not practiced for a long time.

He said, "I'm going to talk to Zaki. He's our captain and coach; we need additional players."

Two days later Zaki Behar came upstairs to our offices and sat down in front of my desk. He said that he vaguely remembered me. He apparently had watched me play with the young teams at Maccabi Daher. He then asked me to join his team's basketball practices, which were held twice a week on the court of a nearby club.

Sensing my reluctance, he said, "Don't worry: we really do not have many experienced basketball players there. You'll have fun."

During my first practice, all eyes were on me from the moment I first touched the ball. I was out of shape, but my teammates realized immediately that I could play the game. Jacquot Matalon was right: aside from the two Behar brothers, the team had no good players. I could tell that if I got in good shape, my presence could benefit the team.

"You'll be starting," Zaki announced to me and the rest of the team. No one seemed surprised.

My competitive drive revved up. I started practicing basketball again with my old acquaintances at the YMCA, and soon I regained confidence and strength. My basketball skills improved.

A spirit of camaraderie prevailed among the players at Gattegno. We had four Italians on our team; they compensated for their lack of basketball skills with their cheerfulness, jokes, and songs. One, Mario Lunardi, offered me a mixed-breed German shepherd, a smart and affectionate dog. I named him Roy. I often took him to my basketball practices. His affection for me grew deeper after I saved his life. One night, while Tante Marie prepared dinner, Roy gobbled up a large piece of raw meat that had fallen from the kitchen counter. He began suffocating. When I heard Tante Marie's screams, I ran into the kitchen to find him choking. I opened his jaw and stuck my hand deep in his throat and pulled out the piece of meat, a good part of which had lodged in his esophagus and was about to kill him. Roy did not budge throughout the whole ordeal. He looked at me with grateful eyes and did not stop licking the hand that had saved him. After that Roy followed me everywhere, even to my bed when I went to sleep.

Zaki Behar was right—I enjoyed being part of the team. But playing with Bertie was another story. I was a more versatile player than he, so Zaki, eager to win the game, often passed me the ball. Bertie began whining and whispering to his brother in Ladino, a language that wasn't completely foreign to me. He asked Zaki to pass the ball to him and not so much to me.

Once, during a time-out, when Bertie whined more persistently than usual, Zaki became angry and responded in Ladino loudly enough for me to hear him say, "I can't ignore him. He plays better than you."

Bertie kept quiet for the rest of the game.

Nothing consolidates and strengthens a team's morale more than success. We won game after game; we beat teams that had always beaten us in the past. Even Bertie was cheerful and happy. We reached the finals that first year but lost to a more skillful team. A few months later the second tournament began. All Gattegno's players could participate except Zaki and Bertie Behar. I was the playmaker, and the team relied on me to win the games. We won the championship. All our top management came to the finals and watched us receive the trophy. My brother Léon led the cheers and encouragement with his loud, high-pitched voice. Silvio Gattegno invited him to the store to receive a special discount whenever he wanted.

* * *

For a long time I continued to experience sporadic abdominal pains. Doctors could not figure out what was causing my symptoms, so I stopped visiting them. I managed to handle the unpredictable, acute pains during office hours by waiting in the restroom until they passed. One day, during a serious episode, I asked Paul Somek for permission to go home. He noticed my pale, perspiring face, so I explained the situation to him and asserted that it was nothing serious.

When I told him no doctor could find the root of my problem, he immediately said, "Go and see Dr. Hassid. His office is on this street, not far away; the company will pick up the bill." He put his hand on my shoulder. "Go there tomorrow. Don't wait. I'll call him; he knows me well."

The next day I brought my X-rays and records to Dr. Hassid. He examined me, took the X-rays, and went into a room in the back of his office.

After some time I heard him shout, "It is a stone! You have a stone in your right kidney!"

He asked me to join him in the back room. With a pencil he pointed to a little white dot on the illuminated X-ray. "Here it is; if you look carefully, you can see it. It is a stone the size of a wheat grain. It's very sharp and irritates your blood vessels every time it moves."

When I followed the point of his pencil, I could see it. The other doctors had not detected it, probably because it was too small and they were thinking of more complex and rare illnesses. Dr. Hassid did not think that I should have an operation; he said that I should be able to get rid of it naturally.

"Drink lots of fluids," he said, and as I left his office, he added, "Your sports activities will accelerate the process."

I was happy to know that the cause of my pain was not serious. I felt more confident and increased my workouts and training sessions. I followed Dr. Hassid's advice and drank fluids often.

One evening while using the bathroom, I heard a soft *clink*. I looked, and I had passed the stone. It was just as Dr. Hassid had described it: a sharp little brown grain of wheat. I woke my father and Tante Marie, screaming, "We got it! We got it!"

In his underwear my father rushed out of bed, jumping with joy. He went to a cabinet and took out the bottle of Metaxa special reserve—a Greek brandy—that he kept exclusively for special occasions.

"Here," he announced, handing me a glass: *Stin iyassou, pedhimou* ("To your health, my son").

* * *

My job at Gattegno had become routine. I could not entertain great ambitions. Every employee seemed destined to keep his position forever. Members of the Gattegno family held most of the management jobs. All employees seemed to understand the status quo and accept it. This was not the work to which I had aspired while in school. I had given up my dreams. My new philosophy was that, for the moment, I would enjoy life without worrying about the future.

One day one of Maurice Samama's friends, who knew I was an avid reader, lent me a book, *The Gambler* by Fyodor

Dostoyevsky. Maurice's friend said it was too boring and too complicated for him. I had read *Crime and Punishment*, and I liked the psychological treatment of the characters and the way Dostoyevsky penetrated deep into their minds and emotions. After I read *The Gambler*, I wanted to experience the thrill and suspense associated with gambling, the way Dostoyevsky had described it in the novel. I waited until the end of the year, when I received my year-end bonus, to tell Elie Masri that I wanted to go to the casino at l'Auberge des Pyramides, Cairo's trendiest entertainment venue. Elie liked the idea, and we decided to go on the following Saturday so that we could rest that Sunday.

L'Auberge des Pyramides had a well-reviewed restaurant and a modern nightclub featuring entertainment brought from Europe and Latin America. Elie and I were excited and nervous about our first visit to the casino, a high-class establishment way beyond our means. We spent some time walking around, admiring the casino's luxurious decor. We stopped at the baccarat table and watched older people in tuxedos and long, glittering dresses as they gambled.

We moved on to a large, crowded room filled with numerous roulette tables and gamblers of all ages who were dressed both formally and casually. As I recalled the description of the characters in Dostoyevsky's book, I tried to guess which of the gamblers might be as addicted as the one in the novel. Was anyone so desperate that he might commit suicide?

Elie had already placed chips on a green felt table. I found a spot that I liked at a different table. To get the full thrill of gambling, I wanted to be as far away from Elie as possible. I wanted no distractions. I wanted to feel the same agonizing emotions as Dostoyevsky's gambler. The croupier, a self-confident young man, made the calls in French.

I had exchanged my entire bonus for a pile of chips that I kept in front of me. All I held in reserve was some change to pay for our taxi home. The croupier persistently eyed me, apparently sensing that this was my first gambling experience. He must have noticed my hesitation. Torn between the fear of losing my small fortune and the strong desire to feel the thrill of gambling, I finally decided to place a few chips on the black 6, since 66 was my lucky basketball number at Gattegno. I kept increasing my bets with the conviction that the number 6 was bound to show up, but it did not.

Finally, in desperation, I put every chip I had left on black 6. This was it; I was sweating profusely and breathing hard. The croupier fixed his eyes on me even more glaringly.

He announced, *Rien ne va plus* ("No further bets").

Then everything happened in a blur. I saw the little ball slow down and stop on the black 8, on which I thought no one had placed a bet. With my head down and my shoulders sagging, I started walking slowly away from the table.

I heard the croupier call me: "Monsieur, in the blue shirt—please pick up your chips."

I was astonished. The croupier pointed at a pile of chips about three times the size of the one I had started with. I was confused; I knew for sure that I had placed all my remaining chips on number 6. Did I place them by mistake on number 8? The croupier gave me no time to think.

He put the chips in front of me, brought his face close to mine, and whispered, "Sardas, take them and leave!"

I took the chips and left the table. Who was this man? And how did he know my name? I looked at him from a distance; I did not know him. I did not leave, though; I went to another roulette table, far away from that one, where I was sure the croupier could not see me.

I lost a large portion of my chips at that roulette table. Then, feeling more daring, I decided to experiment with baccarat. I did not care that I was dressed informally. I had one idea in mind: to gamble. I wanted to feel that thrill every time I placed chips on the green felt and awaited the result.

I ended up losing all my money that evening. Though mentally exhausted from the intense emotions, I felt content. I had treated myself to a trip into an unknown world, and for one night I felt the thrills and uncertainties of an addicted gambler. I looked for Elie and found him at the same table where I had left him earlier. He was no longer gambling; he was watching. I smiled at him, and he smiled in return.

I said, "I lost everything."

"Me, too," he replied, and we laughed loudly in the middle of the casino.

On our way out I glanced at the croupier who had handed me my chips, busy at his roulette table. I never found out who he was. We left the Auberge at about five or six in the morning and gave our address to the taxi driver.

"Let's have a coffee and a doughnut," I suggested.

Elie wondered whether we had enough money.

I said, "Let's count what we have left and save some money for coffee."

We told the taxi driver to stop when the meter reached a certain amount. He stopped in front of a coffee shop, where we had hot coffee and fresh doughnuts. No cup of coffee or doughnut ever tasted so good. We walked the rest of the way home and watched the last stars fading at sunrise. I was happy and relieved, but I have never again felt the desire to gamble. I lost it that night at l'Auberge des Pyramides.

CHAPTER 4

Zouzi Harari, the superstar of the Maccabi basketball team, was back in Egypt. Zouzi, who had done much to popularize basketball in the country, had played on the 1947 national team and helped make it one of the top teams in the entire Mediterranean basin. He played for Egypt at the 1952 Olympics in Helsinki and was a hero to Jewish youth. But then he had to leave those honors behind because of the hostilities that followed the Arab-Israeli war, which caused the shutdown of Maccabi's facilities in Daher. He went to Brazil to start a business with his brothers, but he was an unknown there and was not recognized for his achievements. He soon decided to return to Egypt and to basketball, his passion. He was determined to resurrect the glory days of his beloved Maccabi team.

Zaki Behar told me about Zouzi's return after a basketball practice with the Gattegno team. Zouzi had already met with some members of the Jewish Federation and decided to use the sports facilities of the Jewish Community School,

Zouzi Harari dribbling the ball during the championship game against the Egyptian army in 1953

where I had studied for the baccalaureate, as Maccabi's basketball home base.

Zouzi needed our help to recruit players. We planned to form three basketball teams for men and one for women, all sponsored by the Jewish Federation. The three men's teams would consist of a first, second, and third division to ensure a constant flow of skilled players.

I felt nostalgic when I entered the school I had attended a few years earlier. The school had closed, but the basketball courts were clean and well maintained. A large oval track encircled them. We scrimmaged and ended our first practice by running laps. Zouzi was not in good physical condition. He had gained weight in Brazil, which he acknowledged when we gathered in the locker room for a meeting.

"As you can tell, I am out of shape."

His comment was met with loud laughter, and he immediately added, "Yes, but most of you are not in great shape, either. We all need to substantially improve our physical condition and skills to compete in next year's tournament. Just imagine us playing in our present condition against the Egyptian army. We would be the laughingstock of the city."

He paused and looked at us, weighing the impact of his words. The Egyptian army basketball team was one of the best, if not the best, in Egypt. It included players like Albert Fahmy Tadros, who, despite being a Coptic Christian, held a high rank in the army, which was mostly made up of Muslims. He was a point guard, a playmaker. Hussein Kamal Montasser, another member of the team, was an officer and a formidable athlete—almost seven feet tall, with long arms and legs. He was a power forward, a tremendous rebounder, scoring all his points in the paint.

Zouzi's remarks about our readiness, though realistic, were quite discouraging. He noticed our dismay and immediately changed his tone. "But we can beat the army team," he said forcefully. "We have to practice hard. We may never match our opponents athletically, but we can beat them with smart, strategic teamwork. Our team will have to function as a well-oiled machine." I absorbed every word that Zouzi said, and I believed we could dethrone the army team and become the best team in Egypt. I felt proud to be in the group that would rebuild the Maccabi club.

Our team started with around twelve players at various skill levels. I was far from the best, but I was one of the most physically fit. We practiced almost every night and most weekends. We contacted all the Jewish basketball players who played on school teams and for other clubs. We also signed up young players from English, American, and French schools.

Zouzi had had the opportunity to learn many plays from Neal Harris, the longtime head coach at Albright College in Reading, Pennsylvania. Harris had trained the players selected for the Egyptian basketball team at the 1952 Olympic Games. Zouzi, one of the best players on the team, had established a good relationship with the American coach. He filled up an entire notebook with the various plays and drills that comprised American strategies at the time. This notebook proved fundamental to our training. We practiced Harris's drills for hours every day. We were obsessed with attaining perfection and executing our drills instinctively. Zouzi, the uncontested best and most knowledgeable basketball player in the group, took over the roles of playmaker, captain, and coach of our first-ranked team.

Although I had assumed those roles at school and on the second team at Gattegno, my basketball skills and my height did not qualify me to be a starter. I was a reserve and spent more time warming the bench than playing official games. Zouzi sensed my disappointment and asked me to take charge of the second-division team and do for them what he was doing for the first division. He also asked me to continue practicing with the first division. In addition, I agreed to train and coach the next generation of players on our third-division team. I spent many hours on my Maccabi duties, which, in addition to our basketball activities at Gattegno, often sent me home late at night, exhausted but satisfied with my leadership roles.

Maccabi's second division performed well. As the coach and captain, I worried initially because several players came from wealthy families. We thought those players were spoiled brats. When they arrived at the club for the first practice in their large American cars and spoke fluent English, we were shocked. We all thought that they would not last long under a strict training regimen. They surprised us with their dedication and their desire to learn. They attended all training sessions and were the most disciplined players on our team.

Eventually the team's determination and hard work began to pay off. We soon ranked among the top teams in every division. Then in 1953, our first-division team made the finals. We would compete for the championship against our nemesis, the unbeatable Egyptian army, with its famous captain, Albert Fahmy Tadros, and its athletic superstar, Hussein Kamal Montasser. The hostile situation for the Jews did not sway our determination to beat them.

The game was held on Saturday evening, December 5, 1953, before a sold-out crowd. Electrifying excitement filled the stadium at the YMMA—the Young Men's Muslim Association—and showed on the spectators' faces. From my seat in the stands, I could see that Maccabi fans were far outnumbered by Egyptian army officers and soldiers. A large number of Islamic clergy, identifiable because of their long beards and turbans, also watched. To this day I cannot understand the temerity or the foolishness of our actions. We were in hostile territory; our uniforms were blue-and-white, like the Israeli flag, and our fans were yelling loudly in Hebrew, *Kadima, kadima, Maccabi* ("Go, go, Maccabi").

During the game Zouzi orchestrated all the strategic moves we had practiced so many times. Our Maccabi team outmaneuvered our more athletic opponent. The long hours of practice and training bore fruit. Maccabi was winning the game, about to take the championship. I was ecstatic; it was as though I were watching a miracle.

We were leading by four points with less than a minute left to play. Our victory was certain, and our fans had started to celebrate. Suddenly the lights went off. The entire court and arena fell into total darkness. The confusion was overwhelming. People ran in all directions, and the game was suspended. We had to go home without knowing the outcome. A few days later the Egyptian Basketball Federation decided that the two teams would play the length of time remaining in the game for the championship. Only the players and officials who had been on the court when the lights went off were allowed in the arena.

The contest took place in a quiet and strange atmosphere. A group of Egyptian police and military officers guarded the door to make sure no intruders or fans would sneak in. The referee gave the ball to our team, and we managed to keep it for the crucial few seconds. When the whistle blew, signaling the game was over, the Egyptian military team left hastily. Zouzi received the trophy and held it with pride. The impossible dream was achieved! Our team had little time to celebrate, because our players were asked to leave the premises immediately. It was a bizarre championship.

A few days later the Jewish community decided to have a real celebration. Each player was given an official invitation to the victory party at a well-known nightclub in Heliopolis, a Cairo suburb. We were extremely impressed by the facility. A live band and a crooner were on hand to lead the celebration.

Whenever we would plan parties or an outing, Zouzi used to joke with us by saying in Arabic, *Ha yehsal* ("It's going to happen"). This time he took the microphone and said just one word: *Hassal!* ("It happened!")

We roared. Zouzi returned to his seat, and the crooner and the band launched into our Maccabi song.

After dinner the band started playing slow songs. I found a seat in a corner, far from the crowded dance floor, and watched. Zouzi danced romantically, cheek to cheek, with his longtime girlfriend, Eleni. He had achieved his dream; he was the hero of an impossible mission that had taken less than three years to accomplish. Now he savored his victory in the warm arms of beautiful Eleni.

Eleni was Greek, loved by all the Maccabi players and by our fans. She never missed a practice; she would come to our club, take her seat, and patiently wait for the end of practice while she knitted or read. She also cheered fervently during our games.

While I watched Zouzi and Eleni dancing, I felt a little sad. I suddenly sensed that this might be the last time our team would be together. I walked over to the crooner and whispered in his ear that I wanted him to play the full Maccabi song again. He stopped the music, and the dancers stood still, wondering what song I had requested. After a few seconds our Maccabi anthem resounded louder than ever. Our whole group stood up; Zouzi and Eleni came over and embraced me. Both had tears in their eyes.

* * *

For a long time one of the most spectacular scenes on the streets of Cairo was the long line of red-and-black

Rolls-Royces that streamed down Maleka Nazli Avenue every time King Farouk traveled from one place to another. Advance cars, sounding their sirens, announced the motorcade. People lined the sidewalks, applauding and blessing their young and handsome king.

During 1950 and 1951, however, King Farouk faced mounting pressure from his opponents, mainly the new wave of young officers in the Egyptian army but also members of the extremist Muslim Brotherhood. Because the British government held 44 percent of the stock of the company that owned the Suez Canal, it maintained a garrison there to defend it, as permitted by a 1936 treaty with the Egyptian government. But after World War II Egypt saw an upsurge in nationalism, and in 1951 one of the country's nationalist political parties ascended to power and unilaterally revoked the treaty. A confrontation ensued between the British forces and an Egyptian battalion from Ismailia, a port city on the canal. The Egyptian battalion was defeated on January 25, 1952.

Subsequently, riots broke out in Egypt's major cities. The following day, which became known as Black Saturday, Cairo burst into flames. Large Egyptian mobs marched from the poorest and most populous quarters carrying butcher knives, axes, sticks, and torches and headed to the wealthy parts of the city. The Turf Club, popular among British, European, and Egyptian socialites, was the first to be burned, with a dozen of its members trapped inside the building. The protesters also set fire to the most famous department stores, shops, restaurants, cinemas, and hotels, such as the elegant Shepheard's Hotel.

That same Saturday evening Elie Masri, Maurice Samama, and I came out of a movie theater and walked along Suleiman Pasha Street, past the nice stores and restaurants in the area. We suddenly saw a wave of people running and screaming. A large mob with torches was terrorizing the street, breaking store windows and setting businesses on fire. When we saw the mob destroying everything in its path and bearing down on us, we quickly rushed into a small nearby restaurant while the owner lowered its metal security gate. Eight or ten other people were there, most of them restaurant employees. They prayed and begged Allah the Almighty to save them. Maurice, Elie, and I hid behind a counter and waited for the wave of rage and destruction to pass.

I thought of our Passover dinners, when we recall the exodus of the Jews from Egypt. To force the pharaoh to release the Jews, God brought death to the Egyptians' firstborn sons. According to the Passover Haggadah, the Angel of Death afflicted only Egyptian homes and "passed over" the Jewish ones. I always felt uneasy when this passage was read during our family seder. Nevertheless, it was one of the first things that came to mind as I crouched down, hoping the Angel of Death would pass over our little restaurant. After a couple of hours the street grew quiet; we no longer heard loud screams or the sounds of people running. The owner opened the door cautiously and signaled that it was safe to leave. Amazingly, an empty taxi passed us, and we flagged it down.

"Maleka Nazli Street or Farouk Avenue?" asked the driver, who wanted to know which of the two routes he should take to get to our homes. "Maleka Nazli," we answered without giving it much thought, and the ride home was uneventful.

But it turned out that many of our friends had been attacked by the mob on Saturday evening. Several were in the hospital in critical condition. One of them told us he and two others had flagged down a taxi and asked the driver to take Farouk Avenue to get them home. After a few minutes they encountered a large crowd that was attacking stores and setting them on fire. The mob stopped the taxi, and, fearing for his life, the driver leaped out of his car and madly beat his passengers as he yelled, "Jews, dogs, infidels!" The mob dragged my friends out of the car and took their watches, rings, wallets, and other valuables. They hit them with clubs and cut them with knives. The person who told us the story was the only one well enough to be released from the hospital. By casually choosing Maleka Nazli Street instead of Farouk Avenue, Maurice, Elie, and I had escaped death twice in one night.

In the ensuing six months King Farouk tried to reorganize the government no less than five times, all to no avail. Riot police and army soldiers patrolled the streets of the major cities and enforced a strict new curfew. According to announcements and warnings from the government, Egyptian soldiers had orders to shoot on sight anyone who broke the curfew. In fact some unfortunate and uninformed pedestrians endured beatings and floggings with long-lashed whips.

One Sunday at dawn—during curfew—someone rapped hard on our door. Wondering who would come to our house at such a time, I rushed to open it and found Elie Masri leaning against the wall. He was out of breath and had little color in his face; his eyes were filled with tears. His father had just died. Elie did not know what to do, so he had run through the streets holding both arms in the air and screaming, *Abouya mat! Abouya mat!* ("My father died! My father died!") One soldier had brandished his gun at Elie, but when he heard Elie's screams, the soldier signaled him to go on.

His father had been in deteriorating health ever since suffering a stroke years earlier. As we rushed to his home, Elie explained that his father had suffered so much that one night he found him holding a can of kerosene in the bathroom. When Elie asked what he was doing, his father answered that he wanted to end his miserable life. For the previous few days he had been unable to get out of bed or sleep. I didn't think about the curfew as we ran that day. We did not care.

Sure enough, when we reached Elie's house, we found his father lying dead on his bed; no one in the family wanted to enter the room. I had to straighten up the body and cover it with a blanket—and this was the body of a man I had known, a man with whom I chatted every week and often exchanged jokes. Although I was light-headed and felt a knot in my throat, I handled the body of Elie's father with assurance. I then went to the synagogue and asked for the people who usually handled death rituals. Only two people were available, so I agreed to help them. We prepared and cleaned a table and placed the body on it. We then washed the body and wrapped it in white sheets. When I returned home late that night, Tante Marie had dinner ready for me, but I could not touch it. I could not eat meat of any kind for a long while.

* * *

In his youth King Farouk had been pampered and revered by his people, but as he grew older he had plunged deeper and deeper into debauchery, and it turned him into an abominable, obese pleasure seeker. His hold on his kingdom weakened daily. On July 22, 1952, a military group known as the Free Officers overthrew the Farouk monarchy. Farouk collected some of his wealth and belongings and fled to Italy. General Mohammad Naguib was appointed prime minister in 1952; a year later he was appointed president of the new government as well as prime minister. Naguib's presidency, however, was short-lived because he was a figurehead utterly lacking in political skills. In November of 1954 Naguib resigned, and his deputy, Gamal Abdel Nasser, replaced him. We never heard about Naguib again.

During this period Elie and I had not seen Maurice Samama. He had stopped joining us for our weekend outings. Maurice, then twenty-five, was busy, working at his full-time job at the Banque Belge and his part-time job at a dairy factory in a Cairo suburb. We also knew that he had a new girlfriend. So we were surprised when he came to Elie's house on a Sunday morning.

When he arrived, Maurice announced with excitement, "The dairy factory where I work is owned by a widow and her two daughters; they also own a large farm." He told us that he and another man, Joe Savdieh, handled the administration and accounting. "And," he continued, "I'm marrying the younger daughter next month; I came to invite you to our wedding."

He had surprised us again. We called him El Dabbour—literally "the wasp" in Arabic—a name given to womanizers; a Don Juan.

Maurice put his arms around our shoulders and declared, "We will stay in touch, and we will remain friends. Nothing will change." Then, looking at me, he said, "You know, her name is Elizabeth Papassarantou. We call her Vetta. She's Greek, like you."

I replied, "Greeks are very peculiar about mixed-religion marriages, especially when one of their girls marries a Jew."

Maurice laughed and said, "Her mother has been dating Joe Savdieh, a Jew, for a long time."

Maurice and Vetta married in April of 1954 and rented an apartment downtown in a fashionable neighborhood. We would often play a friendly game of cards on Sundays at his house—for bragging rights only. Vetta was a good sport and felt at ease in our company. Less than three years later, when they had to leave Egypt, they needed to sell the dairy business. Joe Savdieh volunteered to handle the transactions and persuaded the family to appoint him as their representative and give him power of attorney. They transferred all the assets of the business to his name. Soon thereafter Savdieh abandoned Vetta's mother, fled Egypt with all the family's wealth, and joined his brother in Israel.

* * *

"Jacques! Jacques!" Someone was yelling my name on busy Emad El Din Street. I had just finished work one evening in 1953 and was rushing to catch a bus to basketball practice. I turned my head and saw a tall man in a suit and tie who was waving his arms and running toward me. I stopped, and when he drew closer, I recognized him: Nessim Policar, who had attended school with me. He was our class prankster, the one who entertained us with his mimicry and impersonations.

Now here he was, hugging me and asking what I was doing. Then, realizing that I needed to hurry, he offered to accompany me to the bus station. We briefed each other about our jobs and activities. Nessim worked at Mena House, a hotel and resort just outside Cairo, as an accounting manager. I noticed he had not changed much. To make me laugh he pushed a false tooth out from the front of his mouth with his tongue.

"Remember?" he said. "I used to do this when our teacher turned his back."

"Yes," I said. "I remember; you used to make us laugh."

Before I hopped on the bus, he handed me a business card. He ran after the bus to make sure I would visit him at Mena House.

"Come—you will like it."

Mena House was an exclusive luxury resort that catered to wealthy socialites. It had elegant furniture, superb restaurants, a bar that served imported drinks, libraries, rooms for card games, and a huge swimming pool. Membership was exceptionally selective and quite costly. When I mentioned Nessim Policar's invitation to Elie, he could not wait.

"Let's go there next week. Call him today!" Then he said to himself, "Mena House. It's a dream come true."

The following week, Elie and I took Nessim up on his invitation. When we arrived, the receptionist called Nessim, who took us to a luxurious locker room and showed us the way to the pool. He picked a table in the shade that had a large umbrella, and we sat down. Elie and I did not say a word for a while; we simply admired the splendid swimming pool with its three levels of diving platforms and its limpid water. A waiter placed a large tray full of sandwiches, canapés, and drinks on our table. I looked around and saw beautiful women in bikinis sunbathing on their reclining chairs. While we enjoyed our food and drinks, another group sat at a nearby table.

Nessim whispered to us, "That's Omar Sharif and his fellow movie stars."

We all knew the famous Egyptian, who was an international movie star and a breeder of Arabian horses. Before he sat down, Sharif waved to us, and we waved back. We spent a few marvelous hours in the world of the rich and famous, a world beyond our reach.

We visited Mena House several times and enjoyed the same treatment and the same routine, except that with time we became more at ease. We had short conversations with some guests and with a few beautiful women. Nessim Policar warned us about them, however: "Be careful—they may have some important Egyptian military boyfriends." So we limited our flirtations to exchanges of short sentences and surreptitious and longing glances.

Elie encouraged me to jump from the diving board to attract the women's attention. I did it clumsily several times from the low board.

Each time Elie would tell me, "You see this woman there? She stared at you."

He insisted that I dive from the highest board. "That will really impress all the women here," he declared.

He repeated his request so many times that I finally complied. When I reached the board and stood at its edge, the pool below suddenly looked too small. Would I miss if I jumped from such a height? I was scared and ready to retreat. If Elie was right, many admiring eyes were watching me, awaiting my dive. After a few long seconds I rubbed the birthmark on my right wrist, closed my eyes, and jumped. I hit the water with my arms, head, and a good portion of my legs and belly. The dive pushed me with unexpected force to the bottom of the pool; I cushioned myself with my hands and badly twisted my wrists. When I got out of the pool, no one seemed to notice me. My belly and the front of my legs were red, and my wrists hurt, but Elie was all smiles.

"It was an amazing dive! Bravo!" Elie cheered when I returned to our table. "You see that woman in a bikini? She removed her sunglasses to watch you. I'm sure she'll want to meet you."

When it was time for us to leave, I walked by that woman to see if she would talk to me, but she did not even raise her head to look at me. My daring and foolish dive did not impress anyone but Elie.

* * *

In the mid-1950s, despite the increasingly hostile feelings of Egyptians toward foreigners, and especially toward Jews, we did our best to enjoy life and our day-to-day activities. We tried not to think about the future. During the summers I often spent my vacation in Alexandria with Elie and three other friends. We stayed in a rented wooden cabin on the Sidi Bishr beach, where we swam and flirted with girls who spent their vacations in Alexandria, as we did.

We especially enjoyed our meals at the famous Benyamin restaurant. The owner was a Jew from Yemen who was known for offering the best ful in Egypt. We often ordered falafel, fried cheese, and of course his famous ful from its carryout counter, which did a brisk business. Ful is a traditional food in Egypt, a dish of boiled fava beans usually served with onions, tomatoes, hummus, and tahini. After spending our mornings on the beach, we would go to a small Greek restaurant for a late lunch. Because I spoke Greek to the owner, he gave us special treatment. He cooked whatever we wanted whenever we wanted it. We did not mind waiting; we were hot from the scalding summer sun and glad to have a couple of chilled beers while he prepared the food.

We often took the streetcar to return to our beachfront cabin in Sidi Bishr after a long night out. When we were with girls we met at the beach, we hired a horse-drawn carriage, an Arabeya hantoor, even though it was more expensive. We enjoyed hearing the horses' hooves hitting the pavement. We would laugh for no reason and enjoy our ride under the clear summer skies of Alexandria. On our way to the cabin we usually stopped at a cart that sold chilled prickly pears—a delicious fig-like fruit—which the merchant kept under a layer of ice in his cart. He would peel them and put them in a napkin for us. He came to know us quite well as his regular late-night customers.

Although I spent most of my summer vacations in Alexandria, I seldom visited my uncle Vita and his family. For some reason they had distanced themselves from us when Denisica became engaged to Silvio Dentes. After her marriage in 1946 they stayed busy with her baby daughter, Clara, and later grew preoccupied with Silvio's unfaithfulness—he left Denisica and Clara to live with a woman much older than he. Denisica had a painful divorce that affected Uncle Vita's health. He died from a massive stroke in June of 1956. Fortunately, a few months before his death, Uncle Vita was overjoyed to be able to attend Denisica's second wedding. Ibram Lévi, who had known Denisica since she was thirteen and who had been madly in love with her ever since, did not miss the opportunity to ask her to marry him when she divorced Silvio Dentes. The wedding took place in February of 1956.

In December of 1956, Ibram and his family, who were Tunisian nationals, had to leave Egypt. Tunis was a French protectorate, and all French citizens were expelled from

Denisica (at left), Ibram Lévi, and Denise in the late 1940s

Egypt as a result of France's participation in the Suez Crisis. That same year, Denisica, Aunt Pauline, Clara, and Ibram and his family emigrated to France, where in March of 1957 Denisica gave birth to a boy, whom they named Jean-Claude.

Our carefree summer of 1954 was shaken when a teenager attempted to blow up a cinema in Alexandria. The bomb exploded in his pocket. After treatment in a hospital he was interrogated by Egyptian military intelligence, the Mukhabarat. The suspect turned out to be a member of a ring of young Egyptian Jews and others who had been recruited to commit acts of sabotage on behalf of Israel. The Egyptians arrested fourteen suspects in all. The interrogations revealed a group whose mission was to carry out bombings and other destructive acts so that the resulting atmosphere of uncertainty would convince Great Britain and the United States that Egypt was too unstable for independence.

Later the failed operation became known as the Lavon affair, for Israeli defense minister Pinhas Lavon, who took the fall and had to resign. The Lavon affair endangered Jews in Egypt. Several innocent men and women were arrested, interrogated, tortured, and imprisoned. Many Jews and foreigners who had long lived in Egypt decided to leave. Most went to Israel; others joined relatives in other countries. We did not have the financial means to leave Egypt. But even so, I did not spend much time thinking about leaving. I was immersed in my work at Gattegno and my basketball activities, which continued to occupy a lot of my time and energy.

* * *

Denise came over to our house one evening in 1955 on what appeared to be an urgent mission. I had just come back from a two-week vacation in Alexandria.

"Jackie, you have to come with us to the Guezireh Club next Sunday."

"Why?" I asked. "What's going on?"

"Well, come and see for yourself—you'll like it. Many athletes from the Egyptian Olympic track and field team train there. The club has a nice swimming pool, volleyball, and racquetball courts. I would like you to meet the many interesting people we have gotten to know."

She was so excited that I could not turn her down. The following Sunday I went to her house and joined Denise; her husband, Victor; their daughter, Camille; and their two sons, Miko and Rooky. Her children were still quite small. On our way to the club Denise hastened to say, "We met a very nice Jewish family; the father was born in Bitola, Yugoslavia, and the mother in Thessaloniki."

I said, "Good for you," and kept quiet for a while.

Then I looked at Victor, who smiled.

Curious, I asked, "So what does this family have to do with me?"

Denise replied, "Well, they have a daughter named Etty and a younger one named Paula. Etty is a beautiful, charming girl. Victor and I thought that it would be nice for you to meet them."

I did not answer.

I had heard about the Guezireh Sporting Club before, because some of my teammates were members. I did not mind joining it. I wanted to play volleyball and learn to play racquetball, a game I had not tried before. As soon as we

Denise, Victor, and their children (from left to right), Rooky, Camille, and Miko, 1956

entered the club, I joined a group of acquaintances who asked me to play volleyball with them. Later on I watched the Olympic athletes, who were doing floor exercises, push-ups, sit-ups, and interval runs.

Then, after taking a swim late in the afternoon, I looked for my sister and found her under a tree with her family and a few others. I guessed that the older woman and two younger women with whom Denise was sitting were the Pessos, the family Denise was so eager for me to meet. She introduced me to Bella Pesso, a beautiful, dark-haired woman in her midthirties, and her two daughters, Etty, short for Esther, who was seventeen, and Paula, short for Palomba, who was ten. Etty was beautiful, and her charming smile immediately attracted me.

We shared the sandwiches and borekas, small cheese pies, that Denise and Bella had brought. I learned later that the Pesso family had joined the club so that Paula, who had heart problems, could breathe fresh air in an unpolluted area. I did not say much that day. After our snack I left to play racquetball, a completely new experience for me. While I played, I noticed that Etty was sitting close to the court and watching. I do not think I impressed her, because I had a tough time keeping up with a much more experienced opponent.

"Well, what do you think?" Denise asked me in the taxi on our way home.

"They seem to be nice people; they seem to like you, and you seem to enjoy them—that's good," I said.

"What did you think of Etty?" Denise asked.

"She's beautiful. I love her smile, but she's somewhat shy," I answered. I paused and then added, "Maybe her mother doesn't give her a chance; she does all the talking."

A couple of days later Denise showed up at our house and gave me a movie ticket for Saturday evening.

"It's all organized," she said. "We'll have dinner at Groppi's, and then we'll go to the movie."

I said, "Fine. I'll stop by your house next Saturday."

Before she left, she turned to me and said, "By the way, Etty is also joining us," and flounced out the door.

Etty and Denise got along quite well; they liked each other's company. After the movie that Saturday night, the four of us had a few more outings together, usually to a movie after having had dinner at Denise's home. Denise's children loved Etty and called her Tante Etty. One Saturday evening I went to Denise and Victor's house, where I was glad to see that Etty had already preceded me. The four of us were supposed to go out, but after offering us a drink, Denise told us that she and Victor were too busy to go. But looking at Etty and me, Victor encouraged us, saying, "By all means you two go out together—you'll have fun."

On our first date we went to À l'Américaine and ordered trois petits cochons, a delicious dessert consisting of three little doughnuts with vanilla ice cream, chocolate fudge, and a banana. Then we went to a movie. We started seeing each other more often. I had basketball practice or games most evenings, so Etty would come to Gattegno and wait for me. I was always the last one to leave after practice, but she never complained. On the contrary, she always smiled charmingly every time we met.

One evening after practice we went to see a movie. It was showing in a popular area close to Abbassieh, where the Maccabi club was located. The theater was full, but we managed to get two seats in the middle of a row.

A few minutes after the movie began, I noticed that Etty was uncomfortable in her seat. She kept putting her hand around her neck. I asked her if she was all right. She said she was, but I was not convinced.

I waited a few more seconds, then looked quickly behind her and noticed a group of Arabs laughing, whispering, and moving their arms. I turned back as if to watch the movie, waited a few more seconds, and rapidly put my hand behind Etty's head. I caught the arm of an Arab man who was touching Etty's neck. I grabbed his arm, turned around, stood up, and started punching his face. His friends tried to intervene, but I pounded them with heavy punches. The movie stopped, and a few police officers rushed in. When they noticed that I was the only non-Arab in the fight, they hit my back with their rubber clubs, which somehow did not hurt enough to make me stop punching the men behind me. The police officers finally separated us and took us all outside.

On the way to the lobby I heard the police say they would take me to the station. I did not want Etty to be involved in what I knew would be an unfair interaction and told her to grab a taxi and go home. She refused and stayed by my side. When we reached the lobby, the police stopped and stared at me. Etty was shaken; she took a handkerchief from her purse and wiped my face. Then I looked at Etty's handkerchief—it was covered in blood. I had scratches all over my cheeks. One of the Arabs must have used a blade or some other sharp object to scratch my face. How could this have happened without my feeling anything? The police looked at the group of Arabs. One had a bloody nose, another cut lips, but none had injuries that compared to mine. The police took a few steps away from me, talked among themselves, and came back.

"All right, we will let you go this time."

I was understandably relieved, especially because Etty was with me.

"Let's go to my house," Etty said, taking me by my arm.

When we entered the house, Etty's mother saw my face and screamed. Raphael Pesso, Etty's father, was more poised and asked me what had happened. I replied that it was nothing serious, just a little fight in a theater. Etty took me to the bathroom, helped me wash my face, and applied antiseptic cream to my wounds. We spent a long time at her house; I did not want to go home while my father and Tante Marie were still awake. Bella and Etty put some food on the table,

Etty's family around 1945: Etty's father and mother are at left; Etty sits in front, with a bow in her hair

and we sat down for a snack and began to chat about our families' backgrounds.

As we snacked, Etty sat near me, making sure the bleeding had stopped. Then we all moved to the living room, where we sipped hot tea from cups. The Pessos' apartment was in a popular Arab district in an upscale, modern building with an elevator. Their apartment had exceptionally beautiful furniture, a water heater, and a large refrigerator, a luxury we could not afford in our house. Etty also had a record player, which her father had recently imported from the Netherlands as a birthday present for her.

Bella told me how she came to Egypt and married Raphael, her first cousin, whose last name was also Pesso. Bella had been born in Thessaloniki, the second child of Joseph Pesso and Palomba Lévy. She was born between her brothers Isaac, who was the oldest child, and Samuel. Rachel was the fourth child. After Bella left for Egypt, her mother had a fifth child, a girl named Solange, who was born in Thessaloniki, at the beginning of World War II.

Bella Pesso's whole family died in the Holocaust after the Germans invaded Greece and deported all the Jews to Auschwitz and other extermination camps. Before the war Thessaloniki had been home to one of the largest Jewish colonies in the world. Bella explained how she had escaped her family's destiny. Her uncle Mayer Pesso, her father's brother, and his family had emigrated from Bitola, Yugoslavia, to Egypt, where they started a business and prospered. He had stores in Cairo and Alexandria that sold hardware, artificial stones, and jewelry. His sons helped him run the business.

Mayer Pesso used to travel two or three times every year to Europe to order the products he needed. He missed no opportunity during these trips to visit his brother and his family in Thessaloniki and, later, in the Greek city of Serres, the second-largest city in central Macedonia after Thessaloniki. In 1936, when her uncle Mayer arrived in Serres for a visit, Bella was about sixteen and suffered from a persistent case of malaria that the doctors had been unable to cure. When her uncle came to her bedroom, she was shivering under heavy blankets and could not raise her head to greet him. He left the room and told his brother that he wanted to take Bella with him to Alexandria.

"Get her ready, prepare her passport, and take this money to buy her some nice clothes," Uncle Mayer said.

When he sensed that his brother and sister-in-law were reluctant to let their daughter travel in her condition, he reassured them. "Listen, it's not forever. She'll return to you after a few months. I'm sure that the pure air of the sea will cure her malaria."

They acquiesced, and Mayer was right: the trip cured Bella. In Alexandria she met her twenty-five-year-old cousin, Raphael Pesso, Mayer's youngest son. Bella was just over sixteen years old. They fell in love and married in 1936.

Bella believed that her uncle had planned the marriage even before his visit to Serres. They tried to bring her family to Egypt, but the war had started, and they never heard from them again. They ultimately learned through the Red Cross that the Pessos of Greece had perished in the Holocaust.

Etty was born in 1938 and, according to custom, was named for Raphael's mother, whose name was Esther. Three years later came Angela, a girl who died of diphtheria as an infant. In 1944 Palomba (Paula) was born; she was named for Bella's mother.

Raphael, Etty's father, impressed me as exceptionally honest and sincere. He owned three stores, the most important of which was in Mousky, a popular shopping area in Cairo. This store specialized in the wholesale of *quincaillerie*—artificial stones and jewelry. The other two stores were in Alexandria, and a man named Albert Levy managed them. One store sold women's and children's apparel and products for the beach, and the other specialized in fabric for curtains and draperies. Raphael had the respect and confidence of all those who dealt with him. He did not like to borrow money. He had a checking account, but he used his bank only to deposit and withdraw money. He conducted all his business in cash. He trusted his customers, and they never failed him.

Etty's father's store in Alexandria in the early 1950s

He told me that when the Germans occupied El Alamein, less than seventy miles west of Alexandria, he gave a large part of his money to a Bedouin for safekeeping. Haj Ismaël, the Bedouin, lived in Palestine and bought jewelry from Raphael to sell at his store. If something happened to Raphael, Ismaël was to find Bella and the children and give them the money. When the Germans were defeated, Ismaël came to Raphael's store and returned all the money.

Raphael Pesso looked at me and said, "He is a Muslim, an Arab, a Palestinian, but I trusted him. I did not need any contract; I knew I could count on him."

It was after midnight when I returned home from Etty's house that night. Everybody was asleep. I rested a few hours and left for work before they woke up. At work everyone asked me what had happened to my face.

As I told colleagues about the fight, Paul Somek came to our office, listened to my story, and then said, "First, it's an undeniable proof that Jacques loves his girlfriend; second, I certainly would not like to be those men who attacked him. Knowing him, I'm sure he must have hit them pretty bad."

* * *

The scars on my face were not deep; they healed fast. Paul Somek's words, however, hit home. Yes, it was undeniably true: I loved Etty. I loved her unassuming, somewhat shy demeanor; I liked her black eyes, the way she laughed, and, above all, her charming smile. She was beautiful and intelligent, and I enjoyed being with her. Yes, I loved her.

But then I asked myself, "Where will our relationship take us?"

The same question must have occurred to Etty and her parents. The following Saturday Etty and I walked along the streets of Cairo; it was fall, and we felt a fresh breeze on our faces. Etty casually mentioned that her aunts, uncles, and cousins in Alexandria wanted to meet me.

"My mother and father want to organize a party at our house so our family and friends can get to know you." That took me by surprise, so I said nothing. She said that many family friends had noticed us together in theaters and on the street. "My father doesn't want me to continue going out with you without announcing it to our family and friends."

I said, "This sounds as if we are announcing our engagement; we only met three months ago. We have never talked about marriage or engagement before; I'm not ready for this kind of commitment."

She smiled and replied, "We can announce our engagement two months from now, next January, so that we can appease my father and continue to see each other. We can stay engaged for a long time. We don't have to get married soon."

I did not reply; I was reeling from Etty's forthright statements. While we walked, Etty continued to talk, but my mind was elsewhere. I was still thinking about what she had just told me. We arrived at her building in what seemed like minutes. I told her that I wanted to go home; she gave me a prolonged hug and got in the elevator. Later we met a few times but did not talk about engagement. I tried to avoid thinking about it.

One evening, however, Etty said, "My parents have picked the date of our engagement party; it will be the last Saturday evening in January. They have announced it to our family and relatives here in Cairo and also those in Alexandria. They are all eager to meet you."

I did not sleep well that night because images from my childhood of poverty invaded my sleep. Was I ready to meet Etty's family, relatives, and friends? I definitely was not ready to get engaged, marry, and have children.

When we met the next evening, I told Etty that we needed to go someplace where we could talk. We found a café downtown and ordered a couple of soft drinks. I told Etty that I was not ready to hop on the marriage train. I said I did not have the financial means to marry. I did not want to have a family who would suffer as mine had when we were kids. I was determined not to cave in to pressure from Etty's family. I knew I had to end our relationship because I believed it was moving us toward a life full of pain and misery.

Etty was devastated; she could not believe what I told her.

She whispered, "But we do not need much to live together; your salary is more than sufficient for the two of us."

I held her hand and looked in her eyes.

"Etty, I love you; I really do," I told her. "It will be extremely hard for me to leave you, but it will be even worse if we go ahead. I saw my family suffer for lack of money. We went to bed many nights without eating. I saw my mother crying when a truck came to our home to pick up our furniture because we could not pay our rent. I saw her work like a slave, cleaning, washing, cooking, and working the whole day to take care of us because my father could not provide for our needs." I stopped, looked at her, barely able to control my emotions, and added, "You know, to sell his fabric, my father tried to force me to kiss the hand of his client, and I cried because I couldn't do it. There is no way that I'm going to take you and our children down that same path."

I continued to hold her hand and said, "You are beautiful, intelligent, and very sweet. I am sure you will find another young man with a better job and with better financial resources. My job at Gattegno has no opportunity for advancement. My salary is not sufficient to take care of even my own needs. You and I would have a miserable life. You will find a better man. You'll see."

Etty was pale and biting her lips to keep her tears at bay. She looked at me with her shining black eyes and whispered, "Why are you doing this? We can manage—I know we can. You're wrong, you're wrong . . ." Her eyes were scrutinizing my face, searching for a reaction. I was entrenched in a deep silence, resolved not to show any sign of hesitation. I had made the decision that, as devastating as the separation would be for both of us, it had to happen before it was too late.

Etty's eyes were piercing my heart with remorse, and I hated myself for what I was doing. But I was convinced that ending our relationship was for her own good. The picture of my mother's suffering was engraved in my mind and strengthened my resolve not to give up. I kept silent, and she finally stood up and whispered, "Why? Why?" She pushed her chair away and started walking. I stood up and took a couple of steps forward, intending to accompany her home, but she stopped me. "Leave me alone," she managed to say before bursting into tears.

I sat down and watched her walk away. I suddenly felt an emptiness and loneliness throughout my entire body, the same feeling I had had when my mother died. I must have sat a long time at the café, because the waiter came to me and said that he needed to close. I paid and left. I walked all the way home, knowing I faced another sleepless night.

"What? Are you crazy? How can you do such a horrible thing to such a nice family, to our sweet Etty?" Denise was furious. She had come to our house early the next day and had brought Léon and Victor with her to back her up. As soon as they arrived they talked to my father and Tante Marie, and the whole group surrounded me in my bedroom. Everyone was outraged at what I had done.

My father said calmly, "We don't act this way in our family, especially with such nice people."

Léon put in, "All of us got married at a young age. We did not have the best financial situation, but we have gotten by. We're all doing well."

They all spoke at once. I finally managed to get a few words in.

"I don't want to have a family who will starve and be miserable."

"Do you love her?" Denise asked.

"Yes, I love her. I love her very much, and that's why I don't want her to suffer by marrying a man like me, with no means to offer her a good life."

Tante Marie, as usual, brought God to our rescue: "God is great. He will help you; you'll see."

Everyone agreed. "Yes," they claimed. "If you love her, with God's help, everything will go well."

Then my father put an end to the discussion. *Nahis tin efkimou pethimou* ("You have my blessing, son"), he said in Greek. He allowed no further argument. That was it—a unanimous family decision. My conduct toward Etty was not appropriate. I already missed her, so I did not argue. Léon sat on my bed, found a piece of paper and a pen, and wrote an apologetic note to Etty.

"Here," he said. "This is the note that you'll send to Etty and her parents tomorrow with a bouquet of flowers."

I did not send the note and the flowers; I carried them to Etty's house. Denise and Victor accompanied me. The Pessos were expecting our visit because Denise had told Bella about it in advance. I was nervous, assuming Etty and her parents would be cold and distant. The Pessos, however, were gracious and received us with open arms, as if nothing had happened. When I offered the flowers to Etty, extending my hand, she smiled, took my hand and the flowers, and we retreated to a corner in the living room. She opened the envelope and read the note. Léon had done a good job; her eyes shone with joy, and her smile illuminated her face. Etty stood up, gave me a long hug, wiped the tears off her face, and went to her record player. Bella came back from the kitchen with a tray of canapés; Etty's father brought out a bottle of whiskey, and we all danced to "Hernando's Hideaway," Victor's favorite song. The engagement party would take place on the last Saturday evening of January in 1956, just two months away.

A few weeks later, while we walked, Etty stopped and asked, "Where are we going this New Year's Eve? What's the plan?"

I was not used to making plans in advance, especially not for dancing or parties, so I told her that I was thinking about it.

"It's a surprise; I'll let you know in a few days," I told her.

I talked to Maurice Samama. His friend Solly Cohen, who had an art gallery and frame shop, was organizing a party at his apartment and selling tickets to make a little extra money and keep the number of partygoers under control.

"Let's go see him. I'm sure he must have room left for you and Etty," Maurice suggested.

The price was high for my modest salary, but I did not want to disappoint Etty.

Etty opened the door when I arrived at her house on New Year's Eve, 1955. Her beauty dazzled me. She wore an off-the-shoulder red dress and a thin black necklace. She was gorgeous.

We were the youngest couple at the party. We danced the whole night to the records they were playing. Time passed

Etty's and my engagement picture, 1956

rapidly. We all counted the seconds and screamed when it was midnight. Etty and I enjoyed our first kiss, which was lovely and passionate. Then we did not stop kissing for the rest of the night.

Louis Armstrong sang, "Heaven, I'm in heaven," and so were we.

The engagement party took place at Etty's home. There were so many people we had never met that my family seemed small. As soon as she saw me, Etty grabbed me and kissed me. Etty's relatives from Cairo and Alexandria were all eager to meet me and welcomed me with profuse hugs and kisses, too. Raphael pulled me from the crowd to introduce me to his many business associates, who were assembled around a separate table.

The party continued until daybreak. Toward the end, one of Raphael's best customers was half drunk and kept hugging Etty and me as he was leaving. He stood in front of us, his back to the open front door, and would not let go of us. He would press us against his chest and bid us good-bye a thousand times. Finally, Raphael grabbed him and escorted him to the elevator.

Before the doors closed, the man turned toward me and yelled in Arabic, *Bakhtak foe El Samaa* ("Your luck is beyond heaven").

His words would be forever engraved in my mind.

The news of our engagement spread rapidly throughout our circle of friends and relatives as well as the wider Jewish community. The young men and women at the Guezireh Sporting Club who used to chat and eat snacks with the Pessos could not believe that Etty and I were engaged.

"You mean Etty is engaged to Sardas? Jacques Sardas? The guy who plays with Maccabi? Are you sure we are talking about the same guy? He is a tough bastard and the last guy we thought she would choose," they said to Bella. They knew me as the consummate bachelor, one who made fun of married men and belonged to a lower social class. They also knew my philosophy was to live one day at a time, so they were incredulous that I would commit to marrying Etty.

Yes, I, too, was surprised about our engagement, but I had decided to not look back. I loved Etty very much, and, with her help, I was going to make it work. I hoped that, as the drunk man at the party had proclaimed, our luck would indeed be beyond heaven.

* * *

My interest in reading gradually switched from fiction to news articles about Egypt, the Middle East, and the involvement of the superpowers in the region. After all, I was about to start a family with Etty, and I was concerned about the deteriorating political situation in Egypt.

One night Etty and I were discussing this matter during dinner at my father's house. Léon and Aimée were there, too, along with Victor and Denise. (Saby and Juliette were already in Israel.) We concluded that our options for emigration were quite limited. Etty's family had Yugoslavian passports, but because our family was stateless, practically no country was willing to accept us unless we had a sponsor who would sustain us financially until we could find work. We wanted to move to the United States, Canada, or Australia, but without sponsors this was impossible.

At that time the only country that had opened its doors to Jewish immigrants was Israel. The new nation, however, was inundated with large waves of people, mainly from eastern Europe and Russia. Israel had quadrupled its population in only a few years. The idea of living in Israel appealed to everyone in the family except Etty and me. After spending a few hours discussing and analyzing all our options, my father stood up to signal that the discussion was over. Before retiring with Tante Marie, he said, "You know, it's good for us to put our papers in order. We must find a way to get a nationality and passports so that we can be ready to leave if we have to." He took a few steps and said, "I will go to the Greek consulate and see what the officials say. Have your passport pictures taken, each of you, and bring them to me just in case."

A few days later we gave him our passport pictures, but we did not really think that it was possible for him to obtain Greek passports for us. My father had never claimed his Greek nationality during all the years he spent in Egypt. Asking to be recognized as Greek after such a long time was an impossible task, because during World War II the Germans had razed all the government buildings in Chania, where he was born. There was no chance that any documents related to my father's birth would still exist.

It was some time before my father brought up the subject again. When he asked me to invite Etty for a Friday Shabbat dinner, I knew that he had something up his sleeve. As soon as he saw Etty, my dog, Roy, jumped with joy and wagged his tail. He loved Etty and would always lie at her feet. Before dinner my father said in Greek, "I have two pieces of good news for you. The first one is that I prepared my specialty and Etty's favorite dinner, lamb with orzo. It's delicious." As he pronounced these last words, he placed his fingers on his mouth and kissed them.

He then got busy bringing the food to the table with Tante Marie's help. He intentionally delayed the announcement of the other good news.

When Etty and I could not stand it anymore, I asked, "And what is the second piece of good news?"

"Well, you know, you are indeed *to simathemenomou pethi* [my marked son]. You are lucky. God bless you. I got you Greek passports."

He went to his room and returned with two passports in sky-blue covers. I gave Etty hers and looked at mine. "You changed my name to Iacovos?" I asked.

"Yes," he said. "What do you expect? I had a hard time convincing them that we were really Greeks. I could not tell him that your name is Jacques." He pronounced "Jacques" with disdain and a French accent. "Be happy that you got your passport."

I felt guilty for complaining about my name; after all, obtaining the passports was beyond our wildest dreams.

"That's very good. We are really very happy. How did you get them?" I asked.

"You can't imagine what I had to do," he replied. "First I tried all the diplomatic and courteous manners possible with the assistant consul, who guards the closed doors of the consul's office and refuses to allow anyone to enter. I begged him and sat on a chair for long hours every day for the past two weeks. The bastard was arrogant and unshakable, acting as if I did not exist."

"And then?" I asked.

"My Sardayico got to my head," he answered. We used the word "Sardayico" to describe an out-of-control burst of anger typical of my father's family. "I marched to the assistant consul's desk; I insulted him, insulted his mother, insulted his father, pushed him, opened the doors, and entered the closed office of the consul!"

My father went on to tell us that he apologized to the consul and explained why he was so angry. He said he was a Cretan, a son of Cretans, and that he had fought for the Greek army. He and his family had the right to have their Greek nationality acknowledged. "And you know what?" he continued. "I took my pants off in front of the consul and showed him the battle scar on my thigh; he even saw my butt."

The consul immediately called his assistant and asked him to prepare the passports. "You should have seen the assistant's face," my father said triumphantly. Then he opened a bottle of red wine and said, "Let's eat." He served us himself, making sure that Etty received the largest and best portions of lamb. After dinner, while we sat on the couch in our living room, my father took out his bouzouki and played Greek songs.

* * *

After closing the Suez Canal to Israeli shipping in August of 1949, Egypt had blockaded the Gulf of Aqaba, a strategic area vital to Israel's trade. In late August of 1955 Gamal Abdel Nasser formed and dispatched into Israel the fedayeen, an Arab commando group that he called "the disciples and sons of Islam that will cleanse the land of Israel." Soon thereafter, the Egyptian government began recruiting former Nazi rocket scientists to develop a missile program, and Nasser pressed the British to leave the Suez Canal—which they did. At the same time Nasser sought continued Western funding for the Aswan Dam, which was essential for increasing the amount of arable land available for feeding Egypt's growing population. When the United States and Britain withdrew their funding for the dam because Egypt was receiving arms from Czechoslovakia, Nasser turned to the Soviet Union, and the Kremlin agreed to underwrite the dam. This marked the end of British and French dominion in Egypt and the beginning of the Suez Crisis.

On July 26, 1956, Gamal Abdel Nasser nationalized the Suez Canal. The news brought more public displays of nationalism to Cairo's streets. "Our hero, Gamal, restored Egypt's dignity by taking back our canal from the hands of the imperialists," the nationalists yelled.

Western countries were outraged. Britain, France, and Israel entered into a secret agreement to retake possession of the Suez Canal by force. Israel invaded the Sinai peninsula, justifying its attack by saying it was protecting its citizens from the fedayeen and thereby regaining access to the Gulf of Aqaba and the canal. Then British and French forces stepped in under the pretext of restoring order.

The nationalization of the canal occurred just days before our marriage. On the day of our wedding, July 29, I spent the morning at the Guezireh Sporting Club and exercised with the Olympic team. The team members were as friendly as usual; the hatred of Jews so prevalent in the streets had not yet affected the sports environment. They said, "We thought your wedding was today."

I replied that it was later in the afternoon.

They smiled. "It's good to exercise; it will calm you down, but aren't you afraid you'll be too tired for later tonight?"

I went home at noon, took a shower, and went to my bedroom to dress. I noticed my father touching the top pocket of my white sharkskin jacket.

"What are you doing?" I asked.

"Nothing," he said. "I just wanted to make sure that your jacket was well ironed."

My father, Tante Marie, and I took a taxi to the small synagogue near our house. Three other weddings were scheduled for that same afternoon. Our family, friends, and colleagues from school, Gattegno, and Maccabi were already

Our wedding, in 1956

there, along with guests from the other weddings. We all waited for the bride. Etty arrived with her father and mother. She wore a gorgeous bridal gown and smiled most charmingly. I was fascinated by her beautiful, shining black eyes and remained oblivious to my surroundings until I heard the rabbi ask me, Etty, and our parents to join him in a small office crowded with books and piles of papers. While I searched for a pen so we could sign the *ketoubah*, the Jewish marriage contract, I felt something in my pocket. I found a small clove of garlic that my father had sneaked into my jacket to ward off the evil eye. I glanced at my father, who stood in front of me; he smiled and looked away. There was no reception afterward.

* * *

We spent our wedding night in our newly rented apartment at 18 Champollion Street in downtown Cairo. The next morning we traveled to Alexandria by train, and from there we took a bus to Marsa Matruh. Because it was near El Alamein and Tobruk, Marsa Matruh had suffered from the fierce battles that took place in the summer of 1942. A few miles from Marsa Matruh we saw directional signs for two military cemeteries, one for the Allied forces and the other for the Axis powers—the Germans and Italians. The cemeteries faced each other on either side of a narrow gravel trail in the middle of the desert. Both cemeteries sprawled over a large area covered with endless tombstones. Hundreds of thousands of soldiers from both sides died on this part of the continent.

Etty and I walked around both cemeteries. Most tombs had no names; several bore crosses, and a few bore the Star of David. We then visited a small museum that displayed the belongings of soldiers on both sides. Exhibits included messages and objects left by unidentified soldiers who knew they were likely to die. The devastating consequences of the war suddenly were revealed to us. Except for a few nights we spent in bomb shelters when we were kids, we had lived almost as if the war were taking place on a different planet. We did not realize that it was the deadliest military conflict in history; that it claimed more than sixty million lives. Russia alone lost twenty million people. The Germans killed fourteen million in concentration and deportation camps.

The thousands of tombstones produced a scene of utter desolation that made us appreciate life even more and added greater meaning and intensity to our love. It also made us think more seriously about our future.

We had a wonderful honeymoon at the only resort in Marsa Matruh. The breathtaking landscape on one side of the resort was desert, with its endless hills and valleys covered with fine white sand; on the other side the Mediterranean Sea, with its clear blue water, sparkled. We could see fish, large and small, as well as aquatic plants and coral. It was a wonderland.

We spent most of our time at the beach. The desert sun burned during the day, and the beautiful seawater proved refreshing and invigorating. The day–night temperature swings were huge: from about 110 degrees Fahrenheit during the day to less than fifty degrees in the evening.

During the first few evenings, Etty and I walked on the desert sand but did not venture too far. At night we saw a bright fire quite far from the hotel. The firelight so intrigued us that one evening we decided to investigate. After a long walk we came upon a few white tents and a group of Bedouins sitting in a circle around a fire. I greeted them in Arabic: *Al salam aleikom* ("May peace be with you"). They answered in unison, "May peace be upon you with God's mercy and blessings." They were surprised at our proper Arabic diction and invited us to join them.

Without waiting for an answer, they opened the circle to accommodate us around the fire. We sat as they did, cross-legged on the sand, which was still warm from the day's heat. The fire in the middle of the circle served two purposes: it heated a teapot at its center and warmed the people around it. We shared a metal mug of sweetened hot tea that they passed around, each of us taking a sip. The men circulated a narghile, a water pipe filled with a fragrant tobacco lit by a burning coal. The smoke filled the air with jasmine and spicy scents. We had entered a different world less than a mile from one of the most modern resorts in Egypt.

The elderly leader of the group asked us where we were from. We explained that we lived in Cairo, were recently married, and enjoyed Marsa Matruh very much. They in turn told us how much they loved their peaceful, nomadic life in the desert. They invited us to stop by every evening, which we did most of the time. We enjoyed being with them. We spent long hours listening to their fascinating stories and philosophies. What a contrast to the environment in Egyptian cities, where the government clogged the radio and newspapers with inflammatory messages. After we were better acquainted, we told the Bedouins that we were Jews.

Their leader said, "You know, this is how your ancestors used to live—as we do. After all, Moses was Egyptian; he was probably born east of here, not far away, closer to the Nile." When we asked them how they managed to survive with deadly battles raging in their surrounding areas, they said that Allah protected them.

Before we left, we went to the tents to say good-bye. The old man offered me a typical Bedouin white woolen hat, and his wife offered a black shawl to Etty.

They embraced us and said, *Roohoo bel salama* ("Go with peace"). They stood on the sand waving good-bye until they could no longer see us.

As we sat on the train on our way back to Cairo, Etty asked, "What do you think will happen in this country? What will happen to us?" I could give her no answer. I cherished the hat offered to me by the Bedouin and kept it for many years. It brought back fond memories of the dark, rugged face of the old Bedouin who so graciously offered it to me.

CHAPTER 5

After Etty and I returned from our honeymoon in Marsa Matruh, we had to set up our new apartment in downtown Cairo. Before leaving for our honeymoon, Etty had selected the furniture and had shown her parents how she wanted it arranged while we were away. Now, as Etty unpacked her belongings in our bedroom, I walked around the apartment. We had spent only the night of our wedding there, and I did not have a chance to look at it. Our new furniture was trendy and in great taste. To get us started Etty's parents had lent us money so we could buy it and pay the two-month rental deposit, both of which were way above my financial means. I made it clear to Etty and her parents that I would pay them back and that I would not accept any other financial assistance from them—a position I maintained all along.

I was deep in thought about these matters when Etty called me. She said she wanted me out of the house; she was going to prepare dinner but was not comfortable with me hanging around. I decided to go to the office and spend the rest of the afternoon there. My Gattegno colleagues welcomed me warmly. Later, when I got home, I was greeted by an appetizing aroma coming from the kitchen.

"I thought it was a good idea to bless our new home with a dinner just for the two of us," Etty said.

This was the first meal she had ever cooked on her own. Until then her mother had cooked for the family. Etty had already set the table and opened a bottle of wine. "I prepared a salad to start, and then we'll have green beans with meat and rice." I heard the deep anxiety in her voice. She waited for me to taste the food. The rice stuck together, and the beans were swimming in a large volume of very thin tomato sauce that resembled a pink soup. I ate the food and smiled at Etty the whole time. "Do you like it?" she asked in a shaky voice.

"Yes, of course I like it. The meat is tender, the beans are delicious, and above all I love you very much." I was of course lying up to my ears about the food.

She kept looking at me and found a way to elicit a more candid answer. "I understand that you like it, but for next time what improvements should I make?"

Without giving it a second thought, I answered, "Maybe less sauce."

"I knew it! It was too watery! You did not like it!" She left the table and ran to the bedroom, sobbing. I took her in my arms and dried her tears with my kisses. Etty later became an exquisite cook. Whenever we have dinner with new acquaintances and green beans are on the menu, Etty likes to tell the story of the first dinner she cooked at our new apartment in Cairo. "It was a complete disaster," she says with a hearty laugh. "You should have seen his face, trying to eat it just to please me!"

* * *

To welcome Etty and me back from our honeymoon, Denise invited the whole family for a special dinner at her house. *Wahashtuna* ("We missed you"), everyone repeated in Arabic while crowding around us. We seldom spoke Arabic with one another, but we incorporated certain Arabic words into our Greek-French vocabulary because they meant more and sounded sweeter than their equivalents in other languages. For example, *wahashtuna* was the best way for us to express feelings of nostalgia and longing for loved ones. It literally means "you turned us ugly and into monsters"—that is, our presence tamed and enriched them while our absence turned them into ugly beasts.

Léon's and Denise's children could not contain their joy as they clung to Etty and showered her with kisses. "Now you are our aunt for real," Camille, Denise's daughter, cried out joyfully as she flung herself into Etty's arms.

Joy was reigning in the house. Everyone was talking at the same time, and the children's screams and laughter resounded everywhere. But a foul odor coming from the kitchen distracted me. Unable to hide my reaction, I asked, "Where is the garlic and rotten-fish smell coming from?"

Victor said, "Well, we wanted to have dinner last spring for Sham El Nessim," a spring holiday in Egypt. Translated literally, the name of the holiday means "smell the spring breeze." Victor then added, "But since you were busy with your basketball games, we decided to have a Sham El Fessikh instead."

Fessikh is a fish cured for a long time in a kind of salty, mudlike mixture. Victor and Tante Marie loved it. But to me, this was rotten fish. Worse, they had cooked moulokheya, a green soup containing lots of garlic that is usually made with chicken. In Egypt, it was considered a delicacy. Denise cooked it because she knew that Etty was very fond of it. But I could not stand the green, gooey look of it or its excessively garlicky aroma. I could not even stay in the same room when it was served.

So I left the group in the dining room, taking a piece of pita bread, some falafel, and a fresh chopped salad with me. I grabbed a chilled bottle of beer and went to the balcony for some fresh air. It was a hot summer night, typical of Cairo. The air was heavy and humid, but the sky was cloudless and dappled with shining stars. On the balcony I could smell the jasmine plants that Denise carefully maintained in two large pots. While I was still sipping my beer, my father joined me. He had a glass of Cognac in his hand. I automatically extended my hand to take it away from him. Because of his heart condition, the cardiologist had advised him not to drink hard liquor. In the past, whenever he tried to drink hard liquor around me, I immediately took it away from him, and he did not mind. This time, however, he raised his hand to stop me.

"Not tonight, my son," he said. "Not tonight." He wanted to talk about the deteriorating situation in Egypt. He asked, "What do you think we should do?" I told him that I was convinced that we had no future in Egypt and that we should prepare our papers and get ready to leave.

"Léon and Denise intend to go to Israel; as Saby is already there, I think Tante Marie and I will also go to Israel," my father said. "And what about you?"

I thought for a couple of seconds and said, "I want to try another country where there may be more risk but maybe also more opportunities."

"And where is that?" he asked.

"Etty asked the same question on our way back from Marsa Matruh. I would like to find out if Australia will accept us. If not, perhaps Brazil," I answered, although I was not sure I meant what I was saying. But I liked my answer. I decided then and there that I would indeed explore these two possibilities. While most of my friends had chosen Israel, France, and England, others from Gattegno and Maccabi had chosen Australia and Brazil, so maybe we would know someone in our new country—whichever one it was.

* * *

On October 29, 1956, Israel attacked Egypt, invading the Sinai desert without much resistance. Declaring that their intervention was intended to stop the war, British and French forces arrived by air and by sea, and the three allied nations' defeat of the weak Egyptian army was rapid and resounding. They won the battle, but, as became obvious a few months later, they lost the war.

Broadcast through the ubiquitous amplified speakers, Nasser's speeches filled the streets of Cairo. He denied Egypt's defeat and promised deadly fights in the streets. He implored the UN, and especially Russia, to intervene. His voice had a high, lachrymose timbre. He incited Egyptians to defend their land against Western colonialists and Zionists. His emotional appeals rallied the Egyptian people behind him. It did not take long for the United States and Russia, who were unwilling to let the conflict ignite another world war, to impose an immediate cease-fire that was backed by the UN.

The UN sent an emergency force to maintain peace in the area. In return for the withdrawal of Israeli, French, and British forces, Egypt and the UN guaranteed Israel free access to the Red Sea through the Gulf of Aqaba and the freedom to use the Suez Canal. The British maintained the right to return to their former base in Suez if a third party attacked one of Britain's allies.

In practice the Suez Canal remained closed to Israeli shipping. Encouraged by Nasser's success in nationalizing the canal and the prompt retreat of the British, French, and Israeli forces, a nationalistic euphoria swept Egypt. Strengthened by his popularity, Nasser unleashed an avalanche of xenophobic speeches. Songs praising him, the revolution, and the army blasted from loudspeakers all over the city. Popular singers and musicians raced to compose slogans vilifying the Western infidels, especially Israel. *Edbah! Edbah!* ("Slaughter! Slaughter!") was a popular song of defiance against Israel.

Soon enough Nasser implemented his plan to purge Egypt of what he considered to be undesirable residents. He ordered Jews suspected of being Zionists to be imprisoned in detention camps. The wealthiest families were specially targeted so that their property and assets could be seized. Nasser ordered hundreds of Jews, along with all British and

French citizens, to leave Egypt on short notice, carrying only their clothing and twenty Egyptian pounds, the equivalent of one hundred American dollars at the time. British and French citizens were repatriated to their countries with the assistance of their consulates. The few Jews who were born in Egypt and held Egyptian citizenship were denied their nationality and became stateless, like the majority of Jews who lived there. Then Nasser decreed that all non-Egyptians had to quit their jobs at major institutions, such as banks, insurance companies, utility companies, and government offices, where Jews held many important jobs.

Large groups of eager believers gathered in the streets and in coffee shops to listen to fiery anti-Semitic denunciations of the Jewish population. The campaign called on all citizens to watch for informants and spies who might have infiltrated the country. Jews were at the mercy of any angry neighbor or jealous business rival. An anonymous letter or a verbal complaint was enough to imprison or exile any Jew without due process.

We folded the Gattegno basketball team and closed our Maccabi Club, this time for good. Several players, including Zouzi, who moved to South Africa, left the country willingly. Others were expelled, hastily leaving their belongings in Egypt as they fled. By the end of the summer of 1956, all our relatives were prepared for exile. Denise, Victor, and their three children intended to immigrate to Israel first. Léon, Aimée, their two children, my father, and Tante Marie would follow. Because the Australian embassy had turned us down, Etty and I decided that we would try Brazil, a country that was encouraging immigration. "We need young, energetic people like you in our country," the Brazilian consul told me. Etty's father, mother, and sister would follow us a year later; her father had to find a way to sell his stores without taking a huge loss. Nobody had set a specific date yet, but our plan called for the departure of our whole family within the following twelve to eighteen months.

* * *

As hostilities grew in our parents' neighborhoods, we asked them to move in with us until we arranged our departures. My father and Tante Marie accepted our invitation. They were the only Jews on their street, and they had already been visited by a secret police agent who wanted to know my whereabouts. My father said he did not know where I was and that I had probably left the country. The agent handed them a note that asked me to report to the authorities as soon as possible. I did not comply, and the agent never reappeared.

We gave our bedroom to my father and Tante Marie. My in-laws slept in the family room—Bella and Raphael on a sofa bed and Paula on a small couch. Etty and I slept in the dining room. We made a large bed with the pillows we took from the couch and sofa and covered them with a couple of blankets.

We took a fatalistic view of the situation; we often used the French saying *advienne que pourra* ("come what may"). Nevertheless we all agreed that we should be careful not to make much noise, not to go in and out all at the same time, and not to do anything that would attract the attention of our vigilant neighbors or suspicious pedestrians.

One morning my father-in-law asked me to stop by the bank and cash a check for him. "I have to start withdrawing some of my money gradually and keeping it at home," he said. "I don't want to attract the bank's attention by withdrawing a large quantity at once." Then he handed me a check. I looked at the amount; it was several thousand Egyptian pounds. I had never before dealt with such a large sum of money. I took a briefcase and headed to the bank, which was a short walk from our house. Before entering the bank, I bought a copy of the *Progrès Égyptien*, a French daily newspaper that I had read in the past especially for its basketball coverage. I bought it that day for no particular reason and put it in my briefcase.

When I presented the check to the bank's cashier, he looked at it twice. He then excused himself, went to a back office, and returned with a man who, I presumed, was his boss. His boss asked politely to see my identification. After checking it, he asked, "How is Mr. Pesso?"

I said, "Unfortunately, he has a very bad flu. The doctor is afraid that it might be pneumonia."

He said, "Please give him our best wishes for a speedy recovery." I thanked him, put the money in my briefcase, and instinctively placed it between a couple of sections of my newspaper. I left the bank and quickly headed home.

A few minutes later, as I passed some stores and headed toward Kasr El Nil Street, a man grabbed my arm. He showed his identification as a secret police officer.

He said in a low voice, "You are a spy, and I'm taking you to the police station."

Taken by surprise, I replied, "Why do you say that I'm a spy? What did I do?"

"You're carrying secret documents. Give me your brief-case, and follow me to the police station." We both stood on the sidewalk close to a building.

"I'm not going to give you my briefcase here. I'll give it to the officer at the police station," I insisted and started walking with him in a determined manner. After a couple of minutes he stopped and asked for the briefcase again. Once more I told him that I would give it to him only at the police station. This time I added, "I'm a basketball player and a very good friend of Captain Albert Fahmy Tadros and Officer Hussein Kamal Montasser. I'll ask them to come to the police station; they know who I am." I made sure to mention their full names to impress him. His face turned pale, and he seemed completely confused. He certainly knew these two famous players; they were popular celebrities. I am sure that he believed they were my friends. The last thing I wanted was to go to the police station with all that money in my briefcase. Tadros and Montasser would have hastened to condemn me. In fact they hated the Maccabi players, especially after we had beaten them in the championship game. I had to take advantage of his confusion and hesitation to persuade him to let me go.

Audaciously, I said, "Here—do you want to see what I have in my briefcase?" I rested it on my raised knee and opened it slightly to give him a peek. Then I closed it. "You see?" I said. "I carry only newspapers and magazines. So do you still want to go to the police station?" I faked a step forward. He stopped me. I noticed that by then he was worried about attracting attention.

"All right," he said. "Give me some money, and I'll let you go." The only money I had in my pocket was the equivalent of thirty or forty cents. I was eager to get rid of him, but I was afraid that if I gave him the few cents I had, it would only infuriate him. Opening the briefcase to take out an Egyptian pound was out of the question. I put my hand in my pocket and handed him the coins.

"Here. This is the only money I have; I can't even get a taxi." He took the money and disappeared. I sighed with relief. I found out that the same thing had happened to many others who withdrew large sums of money in preparation for their departure. Secret police officers would wait in front of the banks. They followed their prey and used the same approach as the man who stopped me. Many victims were not as lucky as I was. They preferred to let the secret agents take all the money, fearing that otherwise they would be taken to the police station and then to prison.

* * *

Elie Masri rushed into our house one evening, his face ashen. Breathless, unable to articulate, he cried, "The police want to kill my whole family; it's awful. We don't know what to do." We immediately gave him a seat and a glass of water. I asked him to calm down and explain what had happened.

A group of police officers had come to his house, which was located near a hotel that the Egyptian army had occupied during the Suez Crisis. The army wanted its headquarters in the middle of the city, in an area full of civilians, to deter bombing by the British and French. They brutally evicted all Jews and foreigners who lived in the surrounding buildings.

The police officers had asked Elie to take his family's identification cards, as well as his own, and accompany them to the police station. "I was in my pajamas, but they did not allow me to change. I just put on a coat and followed them," he said. At the station the officer in charge informed him that because he was a Jew and an enemy of the country, he had to leave his house within twenty-four hours and the country within ten days.

Elie started shaking when he tried to tell us what the officer had threatened next. "I'm sorry for crying," he said with a sob. "I'm not worried for myself. I'm worried about my old mother and younger brother." In a broken voice he managed to finish his story.

The officer had told him they would find him wherever he went, no matter what he did. "He took our identification cards, threw them in his drawer, and warned me: 'If you don't leave the country in ten days, we'll put you and your family in a truck and throw you in the middle of the desert; you'll all die a horrible death.'"

Elie gave me a desperate look. "If I can't leave in ten days," he whispered, "I'm going to kill my family and then kill myself."

"Nobody is going to kill anybody. Come with me," I told Elie. "You need a good hot bath, a shot of Cognac, and a *massage Sardassique*"—a term my friends and family used to describe my special massages. Elie gave me a faint smile and followed me. I filled the tub with hot water, helped him undress, and watched him relax in the tub for a good half hour.

Then I took him to the bedroom and rubbed his body with paraffin and talcum powder. I poured two glasses of Cognac and raised mine in a toast.

"*L'chaim*—to life. We do not allow suicide in our religion and certainly not in this house," I said.

"Then what am I supposed to do?" he asked.

"Your family will come and stay with us, and we'll have to find you a country where you can go with your family. Nobody is staying in Egypt anymore."

When we returned to the dining room, everyone cheered when they saw Elie's relaxed face. They hugged him.

"We'll have some additional guests tomorrow," I said. "The Masris are coming here to stay with us until we find them a new country."

Everyone was eager to assist Elie's distressed family. Etty immediately got practical. She smiled reassuringly.

"Okay," she said. "Papa Sardas and Tante Marie will remain in our bedroom. My mother, father, and my sister, Paula, will continue to sleep in the family room. Elie's mother and brother will sleep here in the living room—Elie's mother on the couch and his brother on the sleeping bag we brought with us from Alexandria. And you and I will continue to sleep on the pillows in the dining room. We just have to find a place for Elie."

"We have only one solution," I said. "Elie will sleep with us."

"Yes," said Elie, who had now fully recovered. "It's an excellent idea, and I'll be close to dear Etty!" He emphasized Etty's name with a naughty smile.

"Don't worry," I hastened to say. "I'll be sleeping in the middle—Etty on my right and you on my left."

The next day Elie, his mother, and brother came to our house. After they stowed their belongings, we tackled the emigration issue.

"Do you have any relatives anywhere outside Egypt?" I asked.

Elie's mother replied that she had two brothers who lived in a little town called La Unión, in Chile. She used to exchange letters with them but said, "I don't know if they'd be willing to help us." I asked her if she still had their addresses. She did. "Good," I said. "Tomorrow Elie and I will go to the Chilean embassy and see what we need to do."

The Chilean embassy told us Elie's family would need a guarantor in Chile to sustain their financial needs or they could not emigrate. "Let's hope that my uncles will be willing to help us," Elie whispered.

"We'll soon find out. Let's send them a telegram," I replied. I prepared the telegram; it implored the uncles to go swiftly to the immigration office in Chile, arrange the entry visas for the Masris, and put themselves forward as guarantors. I closed the message by repeating what the officer had told Elie: "The police are threatening to kill them if they don't leave on time."

The content of the telegram must have convinced the uncles, because we received a telegram only two days later. They still lived in La Unión. They were happy to bring Elie's family to Chile. They had a retail store in La Unión, and they already had plans to offer jobs to Elie and his brother. We all rejoiced for them. Elie and his family started making arrangements to travel to Chile. At dinner we opened a bottle of wine. Etty offered a toast to the health of the Masri family and wished them good luck.

"Tout est bien qui finit bien" ("All's well that ends well"), she said as she brought the glass to her lips.

* * *

By late 1956 we obtained our immigration visas from the Brazilian government—the documents that would permit us to enter the country. Fausto Cardona, secretary to the Brazilian consul in Cairo, encouraged us and many other Jews to settle in that South American nation. "Go to Brazil, young man," he told me the first time we met. He was always courteous and took time to answer all our questions and concerns. He gave me a few books to read about Brazil's history and its rich natural resources. He also confirmed, as we had heard from other sources, that the Hebrew Immigrant Aid Society (HIAS) and the Brazilian embassy were coordinating their efforts to help Jewish immigrants who had no relatives or guarantors in Brazil. When we visited the HIAS office in Cairo, we were told that they would take care of our lodging and food during our stay in the first port before our arrival in São Paulo. From then on, HIAS officials explained, we had to stay in the immigration facilities offered by the Brazilian government.

When we got home, Raphael, my father-in-law, announced in a hushed tone that Albert Levy and his family had been expelled; they had to leave before the end of that month because they were French nationals. Albert, Raphael's business partner, managed my father-in-law's two stores in Alexandria and handled all financial, accounting, and tax matters for the entire business. He was actually from Tunisia, a French protectorate. We quickly concluded that Etty and I should go to Alexandria and take care of the stores. We planned to leave the country anyway, so we would hasten our departure from Cairo and continue to prepare our emigration plans from Alexandria. Our mission was to manage the stores and prepare them for a prompt sale. Etty's parents and her sister, Paula, would continue to live in our apartment and would sell our furniture before leaving Egypt to join us in Brazil.

With a heavy heart I went to my office the next morning and typed my resignation letter. I had joined Gattegno on December 8, 1949, and my resignation would take effect at the end of November in 1956. During the seven years I worked at Gattegno, my bosses made me feel like an important and appreciated member of management. I was sad to leave and face an uncertain future. Paul Somek took the letter, asked me to sit down on his office couch, and joined me. He praised my hard work and team spirit. "You've added vitality and enthusiasm to Maison Gattegno; we'll miss you," he said with a trembling voice. He then stood and said, "You know, within the next one or two years, we'll all be out of Egypt." He shook my hand and pulled me to him in a long hug. "I was going to wish you good luck, but you don't need it. I know we'll be hearing good things about you."

Etty and I arrived in Alexandria soon after I resigned from Gattegno. Because Albert Levy was preparing his family for their departure from Egypt, we had only one day with him to learn something about the business. We spent the morning visiting the two stores, and in the afternoon Albert and I paid a visit to an Egyptian accountant whom Albert also consulted on legal matters. Albert handed me the accounting books. He kept simple records, but besides the revenues, expenses, and earnings, I noticed that there were many monetary withdrawals. I asked Albert and the accountant about the withdrawals. The accountant looked at Albert and deferred to him. Albert gave me a vague answer: "These are various withdrawals that we had to incur. It is too complicated to explain right now."

We never saw Albert again; he left the country a few days later. I had a few questions about the accounting records and went to see the accountant. When I questioned the withdrawals again, he said, "Now I can tell you. They represent the sums of money that Mr. Levy took from the business. They presumably covered his remuneration and other business-related matters. They started small, but they have increased substantially over the last six months, probably when he sensed that he had to leave Egypt."

I asked, "Why didn't you tell Mr. Pesso?"

He responded, "Your father-in-law had full confidence in Mr. Levy. I hadn't seen Mr. Pesso for a very long time, and I thought he was in agreement." The arrangement was surprising, but the explanation made sense.

* * *

We rented a furnished ground-floor apartment in the neighborhood known as Mazarita, close to the streetcar station. Etty took care of Mexicana, the store that sold women's and children's apparel as well as beach clothes, toys, and accessories. I handled the curtain store, on Souk El Kheit Street. I also handled the accounting for the entire business. After a few weeks I was impressed with the trusting relationships that Raphael had built with many Arabs in Alexandria. He had reliable friends who respected him for his honesty and ethics.

Two brothers in particular remained loyal and devoted to him; they ran a transportation company that cleared customs for my father-in-law's imported merchandise. His being a Jew did not seem to influence their feelings about him. Although the Egyptian customs authorities were notoriously restrictive, the brothers helped my sister's family to leave Egypt. In January of 1957, Denise and her family came to our store to say good-bye before sailing that evening to Naples and then to Israel, where Victor's parents had already immigrated. Etty and I took them to the customs office, where our two facilitators assisted them.

It was widely known that many Jewish families leaving the country encountered serious problems at customs in Alexandria. Men and women faced full body-cavity searches. Customs officials ransacked their suitcases, looking for jewelry. Our two Arab friends reassured us that this would not happen to our family. One of them put his arm around the shoulders of Denise's younger son, Rooky, who was three, and said, "We cannot change the official rules, but you will leave our country with your dignity. We promise you."

When the time came for them to leave, we had a long and emotional farewell. Etty carried Rooky in her arms, and I carried Miko, who was six, in mine, while Camille, then around eight, wrapped her arms around Etty's legs.

"Are we going to see you again, Aunt Etty?" she asked. Etty looked at me; her eyes were full of tears, and she was unable to speak. "Yes," I said. "We promise to see you again, but it may take some time." We waited outside while they went through customs.

Our two friends came back. "They went through with no problems. May Allah be with them."

Etty and I looked at each other and did not talk for a while. I am sure that the images going through my mind were also going through Etty's and that she felt as sad as I did. Denise, Victor, Camille, Miko, and Rooky were part of our lives. We spent so many memorable moments together—what would life be like without seeing them and hearing their voices? We would miss the hugs of the children; we would miss their devilry and laughter. Then, with tears in her eyes, Etty whispered, "Your sister's family has played such an important role in our lives. Denise is the older sister I never had. Many times I've felt closer to her than I do to my own mother."

"Yes, and she's the only sister I have," I said. Then, to win a smile from her, I added, "Don't forget. We promised to see them again."

* * *

We spent a few months in Alexandria taking care of the stores. After I understood the businesses, I started to focus on improving their financial performance. I had early morning sessions with our employees to teach them patience and courtesy with the customers. I joined them in cleaning the store and making sure the fans stayed on so that fresh air was constantly moving. We established better controls for our inventories and negotiated better purchasing prices from our local suppliers. We eliminated several needless expenses. We soon started to show a substantial increase in our profitability, to the amazement of our accountant and the satisfaction of my father-in-law.

"It seems that now is the time to sell our stores," Raphael told me during one of our regular telephone conversations.

"I'll call my Arab friends in Alexandria to let them know that I need their help," he told us. After that, prospective buyers started visiting. Some would ask questions, but some would not even speak to us; they would enter the store, walk around it, look at the merchandise, and leave.

The owner of the store adjacent to the Mexicana was a Syrian. In a condescending tone, he referred to our store as "the Jews' store." Many times, when potential buyers stopped at his store to inquire about our business, he told them that it was in a steady decline. He clearly scared off potential buyers so he could get the store himself at a fire-sale price. He hoped our mounting desperation would lead us to sell it to him.

An Arab businessman who had been a frequent visitor to the curtain specialty store I managed finally decided to buy it. He had talked to one of Raphael's closest Arab friends, and the businessman wanted to close the deal. Raphael came to Alexandria. He scheduled a meeting with his Arab friend, who had acted as an intermediary, and the buyer. To escape the notice of customers and employees, we had decided that the transaction should take place at the Mexicana store, which Etty managed. Raphael and I communicated continually by phone that day, since I had to answer the buyer's many last-minute questions. It was a tense and busy day. Finally Raphael called me to say they were ready to sign the papers.

As I put down the phone, a group of six Arabs surrounded my desk, opposite the main entrance to the store. They had entered from the back door, which was reserved for employees. They greeted me in a polite but chilly manner and introduced themselves as two brothers and their four sons. "We want to buy your store now; we have all the necessary cash with us," the older of the two brothers said with determination, pointing to two briefcases they were carrying. I looked at them. The two older men may have been brothers, but I doubted that the four hulking young men with them were actually their sons. They looked more like hired bodyguards—*fetewas*, as we called them in Egypt. I told them the store had already been sold. "Listen," he said. "We know the price you've been offered. We will pay you fifty percent more than the offer you have now."

"I'm sorry, it's over," I said.

"No, it's not over," their leader said, raising his voice. "You can't turn us down; we won't leave this place until we buy the store." He then pulled over a couple of chairs, and he and his brother sat down in front of my desk. The four young men stood behind them and leaned toward me, showing as they did so the daggers under their coats.

I could not call the police, because we did not want to publicize our departure. The seven of us were looking at one another awkwardly, unsure of our next move, when the phone rang. My father-in-law was wondering whether he could bring the buyer and his people over to the store. I explained to him in French what was going on. When he asked me if I could get rid of the men, I told him it might take a while. "They are very aggressive. They think they have the right to buy the store because they offered fifty percent more than the other buyer. Are you interested?" My father-in-law answered instantly: he would not turn his back on his commitment.

"Fine, but don't come now. They can hurt you." After he hung up, I tried to convince the threatening group that the sale was closed and that we could not change it. They grew more and more angry, and their voices kept getting louder. I was wondering how this would end when my father-in-law called back. He had explained the situation to his facilitating Arab friend. The facilitator understood Raphael's reluctance to renege on his commitment and said that he would take the blame.

He asked the businessman to forgive him and allow my father-in-law to close the deal with the other party. The businessman accepted, in deference to his long-term friendship with the intermediary.

When I announced to my visitors that we had succeeded in canceling our other deal and that we were prepared to accept their offer, they all smiled. The four sons disappeared. We all went to our accounting office and finalized the transaction. That evening, as Etty and I ate dinner with Raphael, he commented, "It's amazing how a desperate situation can turn out so favorably in the end. At the very least, we can still sell the Mexicana store to our Syrian neighbor; with time he may increase his offer."

"Now that we have sold one store," I replied, "I will be able to help Etty, and together we will improve the Mexicana store enough to attract a better price."

Etty gratefully accepted my help at the Mexicana store, because she had not been feeling well for the previous few weeks. She complained of nausea and stomachaches, so I suggested she see a doctor. When I came home that day, Etty greeted me at the door.

"So?" I asked, worried. "What did the doctor say?"

"He said that I'm pregnant." I dropped my briefcase on the floor and hugged her firmly.

"That's great. That's very good news. Aren't you happy?" I asked.

"Of course," she said. "But I'm worried that the pregnancy may upset or delay our departure from Egypt. The baby is due sometime in September." I reassured her by telling her that we would be leaving in June; by the time the baby came, we should already be settled in Brazil. To alleviate her fears I joked, "We'll save money—you'll carry the baby in your belly."

As it happened, after we left Egypt, the Syrian succeeded in buying the store from Raphael for an amount below its value but way above the price he had initially offered.

But my concerns about raising a family in poverty resurfaced and again kept me awake at night. Now that Etty was pregnant, I had to worry not only about the two of us but also about raising a baby in an unfamiliar country. How could I find a job with no college education, no professional qualifications, and no knowledge of the language? Who would give me a job when I had such limited skills?

Staying in Egypt was not an option. I had to face my responsibilities and take control of the situation, as challenging and difficult as it might be. I had to find a way to take care of my wife and our baby.

I decided to take a quick, intensive shorthand course in French. I thought this would increase my chances of finding a job as a secretary or as an assistant manager. I also decided that Etty and I would learn Portuguese in the few weeks before our trip in early June of 1957. Unfortunately, Portuguese proved difficult for us to learn. We found it hard to master its harsh, guttural sounds. And I could not write even a few words in shorthand, but taking the two courses gave me greater confidence.

* * *

We finalized our departure plans. We would sail from Alexandria on June 10, 1957, on a Greek ship called *Achilleus*; after stopping one night in Piraeus, it would take us to Genoa. In Genoa we would wait for a Spanish ship called *Cabo de Buena Esperanza* to take us on to Santos, a Brazilian port near São Paulo. HIAS confirmed that it would take care of us during our stay in Genoa until we embarked on the Spanish ship. Upon our arrival at Santos, HIAS would arrange our transportation to the immigration camp in São Paulo.

Although it was relatively dangerous to do so, Etty and I took our chances and traveled to Cairo to handle packing and final arrangements. Etty's family, who had updated their Yugoslavian passports, wanted me to help them obtain immigration visas to Brazil so they could join us. The Brazilian consulate granted the visas to my in-laws without any difficulty.

Then we went to the Egyptian authorities to secure our exit visas from Egypt, a necessary formality before we would be allowed to leave the country. This was done rapidly, with just a rubber stamp on our Greek passports. No comments were made and no questions were asked about the reason for the trip or about our business. But a few days later I looked closely at my passport. There was the exit visa: the stamp showed my name, Iacovos Raphael Sardas; the date, June 3, 1957; and the amount of money I was to take with me, twenty Egyptian pounds, which I had been given—minus 10 percent tax—in traveler's checks by American Express. But there below the ink of the rectangular stamp were the handwritten words that caused me to stop in my tracks: *Moughadra nihaëya bedoun awda*—"Departure definitive, without return."

It struck me for the first time that this meant I would never be able to come back to the country where I had lived all my life. This would be the last time I would ever see the country of my birth. I was surprised, because we were leaving the country of our own free will. We were not among those who were expelled. In addition, our Greek passports mentioned very clearly that they were valid for traveling, *with* return privileges, to Greece, Egypt, Brazil, and western Europe. Yes, I wanted to leave Egypt because of its hostility toward foreigners and especially toward Jews. I thought the decision to emigrate was one I had to make to secure the future and safety of my family. It was the right decision, but I did not know it was considered irrevocable. When I was getting the exit visa, it didn't occur to me to check whether the Egyptian authorities would allow me to come back—they didn't mention it, and I didn't ask. At the time I didn't care. I just had one thought in mind: leave Egypt. But when I saw the words "without return," I felt their finality in my heart.

When you are aware that you are doing something for the last time, every sense becomes heightened. Your emotions are sharper, more intense. You try to physically absorb the sights and sounds so you can carry them with you in your mind. I began to commit to memory all the things that were dear to me about Egypt, a country I would never see again.

But as I did so, a growing feeling of outrage came upon me. As much as I wanted to leave and begin a new life with Etty, I hated having my options taken away from me by the Egyptian authorities. What had I done to deserve this banishment? I knew then and there what "without return" meant for me. It meant that I had no choice other than to succeed elsewhere, in Brazil, the country that had opened its arms to receive us regardless of our religion and social caste. Maybe one day Egypt will want us back, I thought. Maybe one day they will realize that they need people like us.

* * *

A couple of days before our departure, Etty and I decided to go back to Cairo to say good-bye to my family. My father, Tante Marie, Léon, Aimée, and their children were scheduled to leave Egypt in December, six months after our own departure. They planned to sail together to Greece and from there to Israel. We invited them to have dinner and spend the evening with us. The entire extended family had a peaceful and memorable time together, aware that this would be our last gathering in Egypt. We acknowledged that our situation was far preferable to that of others who had endured imprisonment, torture, and humiliating exile.

My father offered me a heavy dark green vest as a remembrance. Then he picked up his bouzouki, pointed to the vest he had just given me, and played the old song "To Yelekaki pou foris" ("The Vest That You Are Wearing"). We all joined him. In good spirits, he did not want us to be sad on our last night together in Cairo.

Etty and I returned to Alexandria. Early the next morning, while she was still sound asleep, I slipped out of bed, dressed, and took the streetcar to the cemetery in Shatby, where my mother was buried. I stood at her grave, took a deep breath, and thought about my years at her side.

Like scenes in an old movie, my childhood with my mother unfolded in my mind. I remembered when I whined, asking for food while holding a sandwich in my hand. I remembered how she sweated while washing our laundry in a steaming hot bathroom. I remembered her exhausting daily schedule, preparing us for school, taking us to the streetcar station, preparing our food, washing and ironing our clothes, helping each of us with our homework, and staying up late at night to sew our socks and patch our pants while everyone else slept. I could see her desperately crying, watching the men about to seize our furniture because we had not paid the rent. I remembered how happy I was when she had dressed up once to go to the theater and how secure I felt every time she held me in her warm arms. She had instilled confidence in me when I was a little boy by assuring me that my birthmark was a sign that I was special.

My mother had only a few happy days in her short life. I remembered the old days, and I sobbed, tears falling down my face. When she died, I could not cry; anger, despair, and emptiness had replaced tears when I was a child. Now that I was a married adult, I cried like a little child. I picked up a pebble, placed it on her grave, and recited the kaddish, the Jewish prayer for the dead, which I had learned as a ten-year-old when she died. I left the cemetery knowing that I would never be able to visit her at this place again.

With my mind still on my childhood, I unknowingly took the streetcar in the wrong direction, away from our home in Mazarita. As I realized my mistake, the streetcar stopped at the Ibrahimieh station. I hastened to get out, but instead of going home, I instinctively headed toward our old house on Memphis Street. It was still early in the morning. The sky was blue and clear, and the glowing sun had already announced another hot June day. I had not visited our old house since we left it in 1940. I walked slowly as I approached it, making sure that it was our old number—72. The house seemed smaller than I remembered. The tree that I used to climb remained, though it was not as big and as green as it used to be. Two Egyptian boys carrying their schoolbags walked out of the alley. Their mother, wearing a typical black burka, locked the door of our old house, probably in preparation for taking the boys to school.

Then I looked at the house where the Corcous, our neighbors, had lived. I saw a short elderly woman dressed in black and a younger heavyset woman with light brown hair. They were talking on the porch of their building, the younger one holding a basket in her hand. I heard them speaking Greek as I passed by. They paid no attention to me. The older woman reminded me of Ralou Corcou. I had not seen her for more than sixteen years. I asked myself whether the younger lady could be Béba. I hoped I was mistaken. Slim, playful, and athletic, Béba was my beautiful girlfriend when I was a boy. She participated in all our games. She even used to climb the tree with me. I slowed my steps, considering whether to approach the two women. At the last moment I hurried away from them and from the house where I spent my childhood. I did not want to know.

I returned to the streetcar station, and this time took the correct car. On my way home I stopped by a bakery and bought a couple of doughnuts.

"Where did you go so early this morning?" Etty asked.

"I brought you some doughnuts," I said.

"You must have met a friend there, because it took you a while."

"Yes," I said, and kissed her. "A very dear old friend. I'll explain later; let's have breakfast now." Etty guessed that I had spent time at my mother's grave.

On Monday, June 10, 1957, we took the suitcases that we would carry aboard ship and headed to the port of Alexandria. The two customs facilitators who had helped Denise and her family waited for us. They had four trunks that Etty's father had given us, packed with our possessions, and invited us to sit and have mint tea. We had to wait for Etty's father, who would soon join us. Meanwhile one of the two men told Etty he had known her father for a long time.

"I met him when he and I were little boys," he said. He waited to see if Etty understood his Arabic. She smiled; yes, she understood. Etty's father arrived, and soon after we all headed to customs. Etty's father had to leave us at the door. Our farewell was emotional but short, because we did not have much time and we knew our families would soon reunite in Brazil.

Etty had four gold bracelets on her wrist; she asked our facilitators whether she could keep them or whether she should leave them with her father. They said they did not think she could take them with her, but they would try to arrange it. "If they don't let you take them, we'll return them to your father." When we went inside, we found a large crowd of people with suitcases wide open and overturned. Bundles were slashed and belongings scattered on the floor. When our Arab friends saw the confusion surrounding us, they rushed to an officer and whispered something in his ear. The officer immediately asked us to come over to him and to place our suitcases on the table in front of him. We also opened our four trunks and placed them on the floor close to him. One facilitator took Etty by the arm and, in a voice loud enough for the officer to hear, said, "Madame Sardas, please sit on this chair because you are pregnant."

The officer was polite but thorough in his questioning. We answered all the questions briefly: no, we did not hide any jewelry; we carried only twenty Egyptian pounds each; our four trunks contained clothes for the two of us and for our future baby. We also carried two small sleeping pads and some canned food. He seemed convinced that we were telling the truth because he did not search our trunks and suitcases. He called a woman to search Etty and a soldier to search me. They did so in a respectful manner. They allowed Etty to take her wedding ring, her earrings, and her watch, but she had to return her four bracelets. Three of the bracelets were expensive; the fourth was a fine but inexpensive little chain that I had given Etty after our engagement. Our facilitators would take the bracelets to Etty's father, who was waiting outside. The woman who searched Etty, however, asked one of the facilitators if she could keep the engagement chain. He looked at Etty, who looked at me. I said, "Sure, why not?" My answer surprised Etty. I explained to her in French, while the officer stamped our papers, "Look around us. Do we want to suffer the same treatment that these poor people are getting?" Etty nodded and turned her head to hide her sadness.

Meanwhile our Arab facilitators closed our suitcases and trunks, relieved that they were able to help us escape disrespectful and rough treatment. "You are free to go," one of them told us. He shook Etty's hand and gave me a long hug while he whispered in my ear, "I slipped the bracelets in your suitcase." And then in a louder voice, "Go with God's blessing." Both waited and waved at us until we entered the ship.

We boarded the *Achilleus*. I carried the two suitcases, eager to open them and check whether our facilitator had indeed placed the bracelets in our luggage. Our cabin was on the lower deck, but it had a porthole with a view of the sea. I intended to open the suitcases as soon as we entered the cabin, but Etty stopped me.

"Let's wait until the ship moves out of here. It's safer." She worried that Egyptian customs inspectors were traveling incognito and intermingled with the passengers to catch those who might have smuggled valuables aboard. I agreed with her and made sure she was comfortably settled. She was tired from our emotional day and wanted to rest. I said I would go on deck to see if our four trunks had made it onto the ship.

From the upper deck I could not identify the various loads lifted onto the ship. But I could not resist spending some more time on deck to contemplate the beautiful scenery. Dusk fell rapidly, and lights sparkled in the distance. I turned to the sea, the Mediterranean Sea, where our mother had taken us on Saturdays. She often reminded us how lucky we were to have free access to such beautiful beaches.

I looked way off in the distance, where I guessed the beaches of Ibrahimieh, Sporting, Stanley, and Sidi Bishr would be, the beautiful beaches where my friends and I spent our summer vacations—the beaches my mother had loved.

This was also the sea that had provided me with some of the happiest days of my life with Etty during our honeymoon in Marsa Matruh.

I thought back to the "without return" exit visa on my passport and couldn't manage to summon up my outrage anymore. The only thing I felt was regret. True, I had some tough times in Egypt, especially as a child in Alexandria; however, this was my country, the country where I was born and where I had spent every single day of my life. Even though the government rejected, hated, and persecuted the Jews, we still belonged to this land, and we still loved its people, the real Arabs, like the Bedouins we met in the Sahara Desert, those spared from the venom spread daily by politicians and religious extremists. I thought of the honest, decent, and reliable Muslims like Haj Abdou and his two sons, who defended us from our nasty neighbors in Cairo, the Hawaras. I recalled the Palestinian trader who returned all the wealth that my father-in-law had entrusted to him when the Germans were about to invade Egypt. I thought of the friends of my father-in-law who helped us at customs.

Then I went back to our cabin, to my beloved wife, the future mother of our first child.

CHAPTER 6

As soon as the ship sailed, I opened the suitcases and quickly found the bracelets under a shirt. Relieved, Etty tried to smile, but she was pale and obviously did not feel well. She was seasick. After a couple of hours the ship entered rough waves, and she felt even worse. She could keep nothing down and remained in the cabin at all times.

When the ship docked at Piraeus about a day after we left Alexandria, we enjoyed a short respite. I was happy to see Etty recovering, walking the narrow streets of the port, and exchanging greetings with Greek merchants. I could see her charming smile again. We returned to the *Achilleus* at dusk, ready to leave the next day and then face five or six tough days at sea before reaching Genoa.

In Genoa, where we would have an indeterminate layover, representatives of the Hebrew Immigrant Aid Society met us. They were very helpful in getting us through customs. They arranged a small bus that took us and two other families to a boardinghouse in the center of Genoa. It was modest but very clean.

I paid many visits to HIAS and to the travel office to inquire about the date of our departure. After much insistence on my part, they agreed to upgrade our cabin because of Etty's advanced pregnancy.

We decided to sell the three gold bracelets so we could buy a washing machine. The machine was small and had two rollers that we could use to wring water out of the clothes. It would be delivered to the ship before our departure for Brazil. With money left over, we bought a large piece of Parmigiano cheese. We also bought some canned food and a bottle of Cognac. That way we could celebrate our first anniversary in São Paulo. We were particularly glad that we bought the washing machine, which we hoped would make doing laundry, especially the baby's cotton diapers, a lot easier.

After several days HIAS informed us that the *Cabo de Buena Esperanza* would leave Genoa on Sunday, June 30, 1957. The ship would also stop in Marseille, Barcelona, and the Canary Islands before arriving in Brazil more than three weeks later. Because my brother Léon had given me our uncle Maurice Beja's address, I wrote him a letter with the name of the ship and our arrival date in Marseille and expressed our wish to see him. I also hoped he could help me find a job in Marseille. With a baby on the way I preferred to have a job secured in Marseille, close to my uncle and his family, rather than try my luck in a country where our future was uncertain.

Uncle Maurice, my mother's brother, was waiting for us at the Marseille harbor with his two beautiful children. He could not contain his tears. He embraced us and introduced us to his children from his second marriage—Robert, born in 1938, and Mathilde, born in 1940. Each of the children kissed us spontaneously on both cheeks. Their warm reception touched us.

At my uncle's home we met his wife, Odette; she was Catholic, as was Uncle Maurice, who had converted to escape persecution during the German occupation. We spent a long time in the living room talking about Egypt, the war, and our plans. I asked Uncle Maurice if he could find me a job in Marseille. He did not think this was possible, but he gave me the address of his older son, René, whose mother was Ernestine, Maurice's first wife. René had a managerial job at the movie company RKO in Barcelona, one of our stops. Maurice thought I should check with René. "After all, René is your first cousin, and he may have something for you there."

When it was time to go to sleep, Uncle Maurice accompanied us to their guest room, which had a large cross hung on the wall behind the bed. Uncle Maurice noticed our discomfort. He put his hand on my shoulder and recited the first sentence of the Hebrew blessing: "May God bless you and watch upon you." He was pale and pronounced these words with a shaky voice, full of emotion. I felt sorry for him. At that moment I could sense he was remembering the scary days of hiding his real faith during the Nazi occupation.

In Barcelona a few days later, we spent more than an hour waiting for René Beja to come out of his luxurious office. He finally saw us in the lobby of RKO's building. He was visibly annoyed by our visit and told us right away that he had only a few minutes to spare. I did not inquire about a job; I was disappointed and in a hurry to get out of there.

On our way back to the ship I held Etty's hand because she seemed saddened by René's cold reception. "Maybe it is better that I could not find a job in Europe," I told her. "As Dad used to say, sometimes an obstacle is for one's own good." Then, when we reached our ship, I read its name out loud: *Cabo de Buena Esperanza*. I knew the meaning, but to cheer Etty up, I asked her, "You know Spanish—what does this name really mean?"

She smiled and replied, "The Cape of Good Hope."

Holding her tightly in my arms, I whispered in her ear, "You'll see. Brazil will be our cape of good hope."

* * *

The trip to Brazil covered four thousand miles, took around ten days, and was blissfully uneventful. After several passengers disembarked in Rio de Janeiro, the ship moved on to its final destination, Santos, around sixty miles south of São Paulo. We arrived late in the evening of Wednesday, July 24, 1957. We had our suitcases with us and waited for the ship to unload our four trunks and washing machine.

HIAS had a large bus waiting for us. We and other Jewish immigrants boarded after making sure all our belongings were loaded. Two women from HIAS sat in the backseats and spoke to us in French. They explained that we were going to an immigration center because we had no sponsors in Brazil to look after us. At the time, Brazil was coping with a flow of internal migrants fleeing drought and starvation, mainly from the northeast. Many of these migrants landed in the streets of São Paulo, where they hoped to find better work and places to live.

However, most of those who could not find a job ended up becoming criminals; the government therefore decided to stop the migrants' trucks before they arrived in São Paulo, pick up the occupants, and give them shelter in the same immigration center to which the bus was taking us. They, too, were to stay at the center until state officials could find them jobs.

"You see," one of the HIAS women explained in a pedantic tone, "it would not be diplomatically correct to differentiate the Jewish immigrants from the Brazilians. In any case this is the only place you can go until you find a job and obtain your Brazilian residential and identification cards."

We arrived after midnight at the center, in downtown São Paulo. The first thing I noticed was the thick barbed wire along the high walls surrounding the site. Was it there to keep outsiders out or to prevent insiders from leaving? The place looked like a concentration camp.

As soon as we got off the bus, the two women from HIAS took us to a room that held a large table and served us soup in dirty metal bowls; the bread was hard and stale. The twelve people who had ridden the bus with us remained silent, their crooked grimaces showing their disgust at the food. Etty picked up a spoon and started eating her soup. She looked at the women seated beside her and said, "Listen, this is far from the quality of food we had back home, but at least we have something to eat after an exhausting day, and, above all, we are free from the persecution against the Jews in Egypt."

One woman stood up, embraced Etty, and addressed the rest of the group: "Look at her. She's young, she's pregnant, and she's right. Let's eat and thank God for what we have."

The place had two huge dormitories: one for men and the other for women and children. Each dorm consisted of a long hall with many bunk beds squeezed against each other. I walked with Etty to the entrance to the women's dormitory. Half-naked women were shouting and holding crying babies in their arms. Others were fighting over the beds.

I looked at Etty and said, "I don't think you'll be able to stay in this place; we'll have to find you some other arrangement."

"You've had a tough day," she told me. "Don't worry about me; go to sleep, and we'll see tomorrow." With a resigned smile she went into her dormitory, and I went to mine. Most of the men were Brazilians, many from the north. They all argued loudly. I was exhausted and certain that I would fall asleep immediately.

I found an empty top bunk, put my belongings by my side, hid what little cash I had inside my socks, and went to sleep. Early the next morning I found Etty waiting on a bench in the lobby that separated the two dormitories. She was pale and had dark rings under her eyes. I held her hands and said sadly, "You did not sleep last night." She stood, put her arms around me, and kissed me.

She shook her head and said, "No, I'm sorry to tell you." She stopped, hesitated a few seconds, and then said, "Jackie, imagine hell, and then think worse!"

She told me that the women did not bother to use the bathrooms and instead relieved themselves on the dormitory's floor. Etty was assigned a lower bunk that she did not use because urine and feces covered it, having dripped from the top bunk. Babies cried, and women fought all night. Etty decided to wait out in the lobby with her belongings until I woke up.

"We'll have to get you out of here," I said, "even if we have to spend every last penny we have." I was determined to find a solution. I asked her to wait for me because I had to use the bathroom. Its floor was covered with half a foot of water. I had to take my shoes off and roll up my pant legs to use the facilities.

I persuaded Etty to have something to eat, which I am sure she accepted only because of her pregnancy. We had a cup of coffee and a piece of bread with cheese. Then we headed to the administrative offices to find out if they would allow Etty to leave the immigration center and if they knew of any families who rented rooms. While we walked, we heard someone call our names. We turned around and were extremely surprised to see Maurice Samama waving at us. Maurice had heard from an Egyptian who had recently immigrated to Brazil that we were at the *hospedaria*, the immigration center. Maurice knew the *hospedaria* because he, his wife, and their son had stayed there for a short period after arriving in Brazil.

We were so happy to see Maurice! Unbeknownst to us, the Samamas had arrived in Brazil in January of 1957, seven months earlier. After spending one horrible night at the immigration center, they decided, along with other French and Tunisian immigrants, to contact the French embassy in São Paulo to complain about their situation. The embassy decided to accommodate them at a French school, which was closed for the January and February summer vacation in

Brazil. The Samamas spent a few weeks there. Soon thereafter, Maurice got a job as an accountant at the Banque Belge in São Paulo. It was easy for him to get a job there because it was the same bank for which he had worked in Cairo.

"The working hours are very convenient," Maurice said. "I start at noon and finish at six in the evening." He looked at Etty and said, "She should not stay here; I'll come later this afternoon and take her to our place." He did not have to make his offer twice. We gladly accepted.

The Samamas lived in a small house that had one bedroom, a small living room, and a kitchenette. It accommodated Maurice, Vetta, their two-year-old son, Bertie, and Maurice's brother, Toto. They hardly had enough space for three adults and their little son. They managed, however, to provide shelter for Etty. She shared the bedroom with Vetta and Bertie. Maurice slept with his brother in the living room. It was not an easy arrangement for the Samamas, and the friendship they demonstrated touched us deeply.

* * *

Relieved that Etty had a safe place, I went to the immigration offices to put my documents in order. They gave me a temporary identification card that allowed me to circulate outside the center from 7:00 a.m. to 7:00 p.m.

Then the woman at the desk handed me an envelope containing the names and addresses of people who might have jobs to offer—about four or five names, and most of them sounded Jewish. The businesses they owned were mostly small groceries and bakeries, but I had already made up my mind. I wanted to work in a bank, as Maurice did. I thought having a secure job in a bank would give me enough time to either search during the mornings for a better full-time job or hold down an additional job from seven to noon. But first I had to get a job at a bank.

On Friday, July 26, 1957, two days after arriving in Brazil, I took a shower in the filthy facilities at the center, put on my most presentable outfit, and headed for the Rua Quinze de Novembro (Fifteenth of November Street). I had been told that all the banks had their headquarters on that long, narrow street, named for the date of the founding of the Brazilian republic—November 15, 1889.

Rua Quinze de Novembro was about two miles from the immigration center. It was a winter day, during that month of July, but the weather was quite warm, which made me sweat profusely and added to my anxiety about finding a job. I took a deep breath and walked inside the first bank. When I asked to talk to the manager, the doorman told me to wait in the lobby and offered me a cafezinho, a small cup of strong sweetened coffee. The manager was busy, but a human resources clerk would take care of me.

I explained my situation to the clerk in a mixture of French and broken Portuguese. I tried to say that my pregnant wife and I had just arrived from Egypt and I desperately needed a job to sustain my family. I would accept any position and would work very hard. He listened to me patiently. When I finished, he said that they had no openings, wished me luck, and accompanied me to the exit.

I methodically knocked on the doors of all the banks on both sides of Fifteenth of November Street. I got the same polite treatment everywhere. Shortly past four, I stopped to catch my breath. Soon the banks would close. My stomach was upset from anxiety and drinking so many sweet coffees.

Beneath my jacket my shirt was soaked through with perspiration. I wiped my face and looked around. Only two banks remained, one to my right and another at the end of the street—the Banco do Estado, the São Paulo state bank. I knew a recent immigrant would never be hired there. I felt a deep emptiness and fear. How would I tell Etty that I had failed to find a job? How would we live and take care of the baby? Was my family going to be doomed to poverty? Would we have to endure the kind of deprivation I had suffered as a child? I glanced at the mark on my wrist. I thought of my mother's words and of the mark's supposedly magical power. When I was a kid, I believed it worked. *Well*, I thought, *it certainly isn't working today.*

The bank on the right was Banco Brasul de São Paulo. It looked small in contrast to the state bank and even some of the other banks I had visited. I was so tired and discouraged that I wondered whether it was even worth trying this last bank. Nonetheless I decided to knock on its door.

After a couple of long minutes a short old man with white hair opened it to let me in. He offered me a chair in the lobby, just as all the other concierges had. Once more, in a mixture of French and the few Portuguese words I had learned, I explained why I was there. I supported my tentative sentences with lots of hand gestures. But this fellow actually seemed interested in talking to me. He pulled up a chair and sat down close to me. He asked me dozens of questions about my background and about Egypt. He made a special effort to speak slowly in Portuguese, and he used some French words when I could not understand his Portuguese. We talked about the Suez Crisis and the Egyptian revolution. He seemed genuinely interested in my childhood, the kinds of jobs I had held, and my sports activities. Then we spent a long time talking about the immigration center and Etty. I explained that she was pregnant and that the baby was due in a few weeks. Despite the language difficulties, our conversation was more fluent and flowed more easily than it had with the employees and concierges of the other banks.

I asked for his advice. I told him how badly I needed the job. "Do you think they will accept me? I don't know the language, I've never worked in a bank, and I don't have much to offer."

He smiled at me and said, "Mr. Sardas, you are tired and tense. Please relax." He handed me a glass of cold water, showed me to the men's room, and gave me a towel to freshen up. When I came back, he said, "I checked with our vice president of human resources; she is in a meeting, but it will finish soon. I'll take you up to the conference room."

We took the elevator and stopped in front of a large wooden door. The man knocked on the door and opened it wide without waiting for an answer. Perhaps fifteen or more people were seated around a huge table. I guessed that the middle-aged woman at the head was the VP of human resources.

As soon as we entered the room, everyone stood. The woman came toward us and introduced herself; she was indeed the human resources vice president. The old man put his hand on my shoulder and told the group, "This is Jacques Sardas; he arrived here in Brazil only two days ago. He has never spoken our language, but he managed to sustain a conversation with me for more than an hour. He speaks French and several other languages. He is a good man, and as far as

I am concerned, he is hired as of today." He shook my hand and left. I could not believe what was happening; I was completely dumbfounded. Who was that man?

The human resources vice president took me to her office and told me that the man was one of the bank's owners. "He is a very kind man," she whispered. I said to myself, *He is more than just a kind man. He is my angel.* I signed my job contract. My monthly salary was five thousand cruzeiros; the standard minimum monthly wage was thirty-five hundred cruzeiros. I was to start my new job on Monday, July 29, 1957, in the bank's exchange department. "By the way," she said, "your department head is also an Egyptian immigrant who joined us a few years ago; his name is Guido Catani."

After my meeting, in the late afternoon, I ran to the Banque Belge in the hope of catching up with Maurice. I was no longer tired; I felt light, and the run helped me restrain my euphoria. I arrived just in time to see him coming out of the bank and heading to the bus station. He was extremely happy when he heard about my job. "We'll be close to each other, and we'll be able to meet after work," he said. "Come home with me now; Etty will be glad to hear the good news." Maurice noticed my hesitation; he knew I was worried about the immigration center's curfew. "Don't worry. Now you have a job, and you have the engagement letter to prove it; you'll get your permanent residence card in a few days."

It had been only a day since I had seen Etty, but I missed her. When I told her I had a job, she jumped up, embraced everyone, and started dancing while holding Vetta's hands. She had that marvelous, charming smile that has filled my heart and soul with happiness since the first day I met her. Because I had to spend the next day taking care of my documents with the immigration center and HIAS, Maurice asked me to come back Sunday morning and spend the day with them.

I woke up early on Sunday and took a bus to the Samamas'. We had lunch together, then Etty brought out the bottle of Cognac and the Parmigiano cheese we had bought in Genoa. We raised our glasses and drank to our health, to our new lives in Brazil, and to my new job. Etty gave me a long kiss and whispered, "Happy anniversary!"

Anniversary? I wondered—and then it dawned on me: Monday, the day I was to start work, would be July 29, our wedding anniversary. "Happy anniversary, darling!" I said. The day proved a joyous way to start our second year of marriage and our first year in our new country.

* * *

At the Banco Brasul, twelve of us worked in the exchange department under the supervision of Guido Catani. His desk was on an elevated platform that allowed him to watch everyone. Although he knew that I, too, was an Egyptian immigrant, he never acknowledged it and never addressed me beyond casual business exchanges, always in Portuguese.

My job consisted of writing checks for delivery to various countries around the globe. It did not require any particular skill. After issuing the checks, we registered them in a book. At the end of our working day each of us had to deliver the checks to Guido in a folder with our name on it. As I had in my jobs in Egypt, I tried to accomplish my assignment with zeal and dedication.

The bank's salary, I soon realized, was slightly more than the rent for a small apartment. To cover our cost of living I needed to at least triple my bank salary. I had two options: leave the bank for a more rewarding full-time job that would pay at least fifteen thousand cruzeiros or stay at the bank and pick up another job from 8:00 a.m. to noon to earn the additional ten thousand cruzeiros we needed.

Meanwhile I had to stay at the immigration center so we could continue to receive financial help from HIAS, which meant I was still separated from Etty, who stayed with the Samamas. We had no other choice.

For the two weeks I remained at the center without Etty, life was not easy. I did not mind the food I ate there in the mornings and evenings; however, its dormitory, toilets, and showers were unbearably filthy. I had to wake up very early in the morning to take a shower and use the facilities. An hour later the floor would be flooded. I continued to keep my money in my socks because of the many robberies in the dormitory.

I had also noticed that some men hid under the beds with lit candles, played cards, and rolled dice late at night. They were betting the little money they had, and their animated voices kept me awake some nights. But they left me alone, and I left them alone.

Before dawn one morning the lights came on, and a large group of police officers invaded our dormitory. One of the gamblers lay on the floor in a pool of blood. They arrested some suspects and carried the bleeding man away on a stretcher.

While I stayed at the center, I took Portuguese lessons three times a week after work. HIAS recommended a teacher of German heritage who gave lessons at his home. He taught a group of five other immigrants—Jews from

Egypt, like me. He was a skilled and efficient teacher. My knowledge of French helped me make noticeable progress in a short time.

As the date of our baby's birth approached, HIAS officials encouraged us to rent an apartment and offered to pay the three-month deposit required by the real estate agency. We finally found a place on Avenida Rangel Pestana; the apartment was on the tenth floor of a tall building with a concierge and an elevator. The monthly rent was about the same as my salary at the bank, and although HIAS officials continued to help us, covering our daily needs, I had to find another job soon. Many Egyptians who had immigrated to Brazil and France complained bitterly about the way they were treated by HIAS. What did they expect? Despite the bad conditions at the immigration center, Etty and I will remain forever grateful for the help HIAS provided us while we were struggling to start a new life in Brazil.

The small apartment had one bedroom and a tiny living room. The narrow kitchen also served as a dining room. We liked the bathroom and the shower most of all. It was far more comfortable than the places I had lived in Alexandria and Cairo before our marriage. Etty especially liked its location, within walking distance of my bank.

We moved in mid-August of 1957. After I brought in our four trunks, the washing machine, and our suitcases, I took a long, hot shower in our clean bathroom. Everything seemed fine, except I still needed to find another job quickly.

I decided to contact the chamber of commerce and obtain lists of the American, British, and French companies that were members. I drafted a job application letter in French, and I used dictionaries to translate it into English. Etty, who had a better command of English, helped me edit it. We sent nearly three hundred letters, all written by hand in English and French. I stayed up late at night, writing as many letters as I could. Etty wrote most of them during the day; I gave her a thick pen and asked her to write with strong strokes. If they submitted the letter to a handwriting analyst, I wanted them to conclude that a strong, determined man had written it.

During the last week of August we were waiting for responses to my job applications and counting the days until Etty's due date. During that hectic time luck struck again. As I walked down the street from the bank one evening, I stopped in front of a large warehouse that belonged to a Brazilian company. One employee came over to me and asked if I needed help.

I said, "As a matter of fact, yes. I need a job." The man, who appeared to be the boss, laughed and asked several questions. I told him about our situation and explained I needed to be able to work mornings. I was willing to start very early.

To my surprise he said, "As it happens, we are indeed looking for a storekeeper in this warehouse for the early hours. Just stop by tomorrow, and we'll discuss it."

He hired me the next morning. I had to start work at 6:30 and leave before noon so that I could be on time at the bank. He said my monthly salary would be ten thousand cruzeiros, twice what I made at the bank and enough to cover our living expenses. I hurried home to announce the great news to Etty. "Now I can have the baby," she said with a big smile.

My job was more like that of a dispatcher than that of a storekeeper. It required me to stay on the move, checking, filing, billing, and preparing shipments; it was a welcome change from the sedentary work at the bank. Every day, as soon as I left my morning job, I ran uphill on Rua Quinze de Novembro and grabbed a hot dog, a slice of cheese, some chicken, or a shrimp pie for lunch and gulped it on my way to the bank.

During the second week of September, the event we had been anticipating with such joy took place: our first daughter, Dora—named after my mother—was born. When I saw her in Etty's arms, the whole world changed. *I am a father!* I kept telling myself.

A day or so after Etty came home from the hospital, we tried to use the washing machine we had bought in Italy. To our disappointment we found that the wringers were missing. Because Etty could not stand up for long periods, I washed our clothes late at night, after I got home from my evening Portuguese lessons. Just looking at Etty and our beautiful daughter made me forget my exhaustion. We had many difficulties to confront, but our little Dora wiped them away with a giggle or a smile. Within a few weeks Etty's personality underwent a noticeable metamorphosis. She became stronger and more confident in herself.

* * *

We received more than eighty responses to the job applications we had mailed, and about one-third of them asked that I schedule an interview. I decided to contact—in alphabetical order—the most interesting companies, including Armour, the meatpacking company; Clarks, the shoe company; Eli Lilly, the pharmaceuticals company; Ford, General Motors, and Goodyear. Armour offered me a job as a salesman. It was an attractive job with a good salary, a commission on sales, and a Jeep to use within the state of São Paulo. But it meant being on the road most days of the week. Etty and I decided not to pursue it.

I liked the offer from Clarks because its president was young, dynamic, and inspiring. "You'll have great opportunities with us," he said. "We'll train you, and very soon we'll give you a store to run. And from there it will all depend on you—the sky is the limit." I asked him to give me a few days to think it over.

I told Etty I was seriously considering his offer. "He gave you some time. You don't have to rush; you can still check two or three more companies before making up your mind," she counseled. So I contacted Ford and General Motors, but they were busy with an automobile show and asked me to call back in a couple of weeks.

Then I made a call that, I would come to realize later, changed the course of my life. I called Goodyear and scheduled an appointment with its sales director, Charles Jule Pilliod, Jr. The name sounded pompous and imposing. I shared my concern with Etty, who again used her common sense. "Don't worry about the name. Who knows? You may like him. After all, you have the offer from Clarks, and you still have your two jobs. We can manage if you don't find something better."

For no particular reason I felt I had to be better prepared for the Goodyear interview than for the earlier ones. Perhaps it was my interviewer's name. I wrote down my background in French. I described my childhood, my sports activities, the Egyptian coup and its aftermath, the Suez Crisis, our long trip, and the arrival of our baby. With Etty's help and the help of a French-English dictionary, I translated it into English and rehearsed it many times until I had learned it by heart. Etty made me repeat it several times, as I tried to improve my pronunciation and my heavy accent. I was ready to meet Charles Jule Pilliod, Jr.

The Goodyear people agreed to meet me late in the afternoon, after I left the bank. Goodyear's headquarters were located in Belenzinho, a busy quarter of São Paulo. The offices were in a big old building, but most of the site was occupied by Goodyear's manufacturing facilities. Mr. Pilliod's secretary accompanied me to his office.

Charles Jule Pilliod, Jr., had the body of a wrestler. His face and square jaw emanated strength and determination. The first part of our interview was a monologue; he was breaking the ice by describing his previous assignments and his own background. He spoke from the corner of his mouth, barely pronouncing the words: this, added to my poor knowledge of the English language, made it more difficult for me to comprehend what he was saying.

I felt desperate and ready to leave. How could I work in an American company if I had such a hard time understanding the language? But a voice inside me was telling me to persist. It was the same voice that had spoken to me since childhood, urging me to keep going no matter what. I decided to chase away my negative thoughts and concentrate fully on what Mr. Pilliod was saying.

From what little I grasped, I understood that he had been a bomber captain in the Far East during World War II. Goodyear had hired him at the end of the war and sent him to South America. He went on to describe the job for which I had applied. I understood little of what he said. I knew it had something to do with administrative work and helping the assistant sales manager. One thing I understood quite well: the monthly salary was twenty thousand cruzeiros, which captured my full attention. It was five thousand cruzeiros more than my two jobs combined.

Mr. Pilliod then asked about my background. I talked briefly about my childhood, the death of my mother, my love of sports, my marriage to Etty, her traveling while seven months pregnant, the birth of our first baby, and my previous and recent jobs. Then he asked a question about Egypt's military coup and the Suez Crisis. That was the part I had rehearsed the most, because the American and foreign media still discussed it. This was my shining moment. I took off on a lengthy description of what had happened, giving insights into how difficult life was for us there and why Jews and many foreigners had decided to leave the country. He listened carefully to my comments without interrupting me.

Mr. Pilliod seemed impressed with the way I described the situation and especially with my opinion of the events. When he inquired about my salaries, he did not have a negative reaction. He seemed pleased with our conversation. "We'll send a letter to your home giving you our decision," he said, smiling.

Although the interview had gone well, I did not feel confident in my ability to handle the job. When I got home I told Etty that my knowledge of Portuguese and English was so inadequate that I doubted Goodyear would keep me even if they hired me in the first place.

She shook her head and said, "What happened to the strong and determined man I married, ready to face the most difficult challenges? What happened to your confidence?"

"I lost it on our way to Brazil; it got diluted in the ocean," I answered.

But despite my misgivings, we received Goodyear's offer in early October. I was hired effective Friday, November 1. This allowed me time to give proper notice to my two employers. The letter listed my salary as 22,500 cruzeiros, more than the twenty thousand mentioned in my interview. "I think Mr. Pilliod has given you a substantial incentive to make sure you join Goodyear. He was impressed by you, and he really wants you," Etty said. Nevertheless, deep in my heart I was convinced that he was simply touched by my story and had decided to grant me an unexpectedly generous financial offer. A 50 percent raise over the fifteen thousand cruzeiros I was making in my two jobs was indeed a convincing and generous incentive.

Etty was euphoric and kept repeating, "I told you so! Remember when I asked you to be patient and check other opportunities when you wanted to join Clarks?"

"Yes," I said. "I remember. You are beautiful and wise, and I love you very much." Etty was smiling, radiating with joy, and I wanted the moment to last forever—so I vowed to provide her with many more reasons to smile that way in the future. There was no way I would spoil her excitement with any hint of hesitation or negativity. I decided there and then that I had to succeed; failure was not an option.

* * *

On my first day at Goodyear, Mr. Pilliod introduced me to Mr. Alameda, his assistant sales manager, to whom I would report. He then took me around the building to meet the department managers and later on a plant tour. The tour ended at Mr. Alameda's office. Mr. Pilliod explained that I would be an administrative assistant in the sales department. "Your job is to alleviate Mr. Alameda's workload in order for him to better assist me."

When Mr. Pilliod left, Mr. Alameda said, "Before you start your new job, you will spend four months working in the plant to get acquainted with all facets of manufacturing. You will have to write me a weekly report of what you did and learned."

"In Portuguese?" I asked. I was relieved when he answered in the affirmative. Portuguese, a Romance language, was less painful for me than English, and I had used it in my first two jobs. Still, I knew I had to improve my language skills, so I enrolled at the English Institute in São Paulo for a two-year course. I took six lessons a week—Portuguese lessons on Monday, Wednesday, and Friday, and English lessons on Tuesday, Thursday, and Saturday. After the Saturday lessons I dedicated the rest of the day to writing my weekly reports for Goodyear and completing my homework. My workday was about sixteen hours, six days a week.

The first thing I did when I came home late at night, after kissing Etty, was slip into our bedroom to watch little Dora sleep. I spent long moments admiring her face. She had a tiny crease at the corner of her lips—a result, I imagined, of playful and joyful images unspooling in her dreams. Then Etty kept me company while I ate dinner. Because she was still weak from giving birth, I had to take care of the laundry before going to sleep. Wringing out the water was the toughest part. I had blisters on both hands from rubbing, squeezing, and twisting the clothes. To make light of the difficulty in front of Etty, I used to curse the Italian manufacturer who forgot to include the rollers with the washing machine we had bought in Genoa. To the tune of "La donna è mobile," for instance, I would sing, "The man was a liar; he stole our dryer. If he were here, I'd spin off his ear." Etty would laugh and kiss me, and that was enough to erase all the exhaustion of the day before I retired for a few hours. The alarm clock rang at five every morning.

* * *

In March of 1958, after I finished my four-month training in the factory, I graduated to the next stage of my employment and became Mr. Alameda's administrative assistant. The first day, Mr. Alameda said that I had to receive all the mail addressed to him and to take care of all matters I thought I could handle myself.

A few weeks later, however, when I sent a response to a district manager that I had written on Mr. Alameda's behalf, he ran out of his office and yelled at me. "No, you are not allowed to handle these kinds of issues. Only I can do that," he said, clutching his eyeglasses.

"Is the information I've sent wrong?" I asked. It was not. Without further explanation, he said, "From now on, when there is an important matter to be handled, you'll have to bring it over to me. If you have any doubt, bring it to me anyway." I was both confused and disappointed. If the only thing I was allowed to do was to open envelopes and distribute the mail, then I was nothing more than an office boy. But I could not afford to lose my job, so I decided to follow Mr. Alameda's instructions to the letter.

For many weeks I performed my job that way. To alleviate my frustration I gave more time and attention to my

English and Portuguese lessons and made noticeable progress in both. But early one morning Mr. Pilliod's secretary said that Mr. Pilliod wanted to see me. As soon as I entered his office, Mr. Pilliod shut the door behind us and asked me to take a seat. He said that Mr. Alameda had complained that I was not the right man for the job.

I felt the office spinning around me. Caught in an unfair situation, I realized that I was about to be fired. Mr. Pilliod continued explaining, but my thoughts raced elsewhere. What would we do, now that I had resigned from my former jobs and turned down others? How would we raise the baby?

Mr. Pilliod told me that he had mentioned me to the president of Ford in Brazil during a golf outing. "He has many Egyptian employees, and he has a very high opinion of them. He wants to offer you a job, and it carries a higher salary than you make here," Mr. Pilliod said. Clearly he expected me to jump at the opportunity. He handed me the business card of the president of Ford Brazil. "He said he can see you next Monday morning at his office. Just call his secretary to confirm."

Mr. Pilliod stood up to conclude our discussion. I did not leave my seat. I was not ready to admit defeat. Rubbing my wrist, trying to find the right words to stop this disaster, I said, "Mr. Pilliod, I would like to know why Mr. Alameda claims that I am not the right man for this job."

"He thinks you do not take enough initiative to alleviate his workload."

Shaking, I explained the instructions Mr. Alameda had given me after I had started taking initiative. "He did not allow me to help him; that is the truth, Mr. Pilliod," I said, looking directly into his eyes. "For me, it's more important to prove that I can handle the position you offered me than to take a higher-paying job elsewhere. I want to prove to you that I'm not a failure. After that I can leave Goodyear."

"Well," he said, "let's call Mr. Alameda in." He arrived, and Mr. Pilliod briefed him on our discussion. Then Mr. Pilliod said, "Jacques wants to prove to us that he can perform if you give him the opportunity and the authority."

Mr. Alameda asked me, "In that case you risk losing this job and the one offered by Ford. Is this what you want?"

"Yes," I answered immediately.

Mr. Pilliod was not the kind of man who took long to reach a decision. He put his hands on his desk and said, "Okay, we're going to give Jacques another three months to prove what he can accomplish." Then, looking at Mr. Alameda, he added, "You are going to allow him to take care of every matter that comes to your attention. He will defer to you only on the issues that he cannot handle. I am giving him the authority to do so. Are we all in agreement?" Mr. Alameda and I nodded, and we all shook hands.

That evening I stayed in the office long after everyone had left. I walked around the halls, looked at the empty offices, and read the names of the managers on each door. I walked to the factory, where the night-shift workers recognized me and gave me an *abraço*, the traditional Brazilian hug. I took a piece of rubber from the extruder and chewed it as I would a piece of gum. I took a deep breath, inhaled the smell of the rubber around me in the plant, and savored the piece in my mouth. A deep feeling of comfort warmed my body. I belonged to this company. I was part of it; I would not let anyone separate me from it.

During the ensuing weeks, I plunged relentlessly into my job. In less than three months Mr. Alameda ended up without much to do and was transferred to a job in Portugal. As time went on, I increased my value to the company by accepting assignments that were not part of my job—assignments that others turned down because they were unwilling or too busy to perform them.

* * *

I got my first big opportunity at Goodyear in a most unexpected way. One day in late 1958, Mr. Pilliod called me into his office and explained that the manager of the miscellaneous department had been hospitalized after a nervous breakdown and would not come back to work. "It's a pity, but the show must go on. I was wondering if you want to handle all the administrative work for this department until we decide what to do. It's a temporary assignment. Can you handle this work in addition to your current job?"

"Yes," I said without hesitation.

The miscellaneous department sold various automotive products, such as fan belts, batteries, and radiator hoses. The main product, however, was retread material. It was officially called the *departamento de produtos diversos*, but it was better known as the jinx department because everyone who had run it suffered bad luck. An American named Clark died at a young age from prostate cancer. Harrison, the older and more experienced executive who followed him, died suddenly at his desk from a massive heart attack. And the current manager was out with mental problems. I did not spend much time thinking about the curse of the jinx department. I had to get busy and start handling all its administrative work, as I had promised Mr. Pilliod. Once again I redoubled my efforts.

A few months later, as anticipated, a new manager, an American sent from our Akron head office, was named to run the miscellaneous department. Soon, though, he began to be overwhelmed with quality-control problems and was fired. The curse on the miscellaneous department continued. Less than three months after he left, the department lost two more managers. The paperwork and demands of the job overwhelmed the first, and the second died in a horrible car accident.

Without waiting for Mr. Pilliod to ask me, I took over the department's administrative work each time the job came open. My following up in this way came to be expected. I was working late at my desk one evening when I looked up to find Mr. Pilliod standing before me. He put his hand on my shoulder, as he often did. "Jacko, you've been handling the miscellaneous department for so long: I think it's time for you to manage it. Tomorrow morning you'll officially be the manager of the department. Congratulations." I could not contain my excitement. I stood up and thanked him. "I won't disappoint you," I said. The jinx department turned out to be my lucky department. It was my springboard to successive important promotions at Goodyear.

* * *

I rose up through the Brazilian organization until I became its sales director. By that time, Etty and I had three more daughters: Marianne, born in 1958; Isabela, born in 1962; and Claudia, born in 1963. Each of our four beautiful daughters had her own personality. Dora was the intellectual: she

Chuck Pilliod gives me my five-year pin at Goodyear in Brazil, 1962

loved reading, listening to classical music, and playing the piano. Marianne was the artist: she amazed us with her paintings and her proficiency at ballet. Isabela was the reflective one—the most organized and the peacekeeper in the family. Claudia was the devilish one, always up to some madcap activity. They also liked sports, including swimming, horseback riding, hiking, and running. The four of them filled our home with songs, screams, and laughter. They also filled our hearts with love and happiness.

My job at Goodyear Brazil required me to travel several times to our corporate headquarters in Akron, Ohio. It was while I was on one of these trips that I decided to extend my stay abroad and visit my family in Israel. On my last day there, my father and Tante Marie wanted me to come to their home near Tel Aviv for lunch. Dad made two of his specialties—his orzo and lamb and an avgolemono soup, prepared with chicken, eggs, and lemon. My father kept filling my plate and exclaiming repeatedly how happy he was to see me enjoying his food. When the time came to leave, he asked me to wait a few minutes. He went to his bedroom. When he came back, he slipped into my pocket a card that he had written.

"Take this and keep it always close to your heart." He then led me to a door, positioned me beneath a mezuzah, and blessed me the way he always had done in Egypt. He hugged me as if he did not want to let me go. He and Tante Marie had tears in their eyes as I got into a taxi to go to the airport.

After I took my seat on the plane, I opened and read the card my father had handed me. It was a farewell note. He felt sure we would not see each other again, but he wanted me to know how much he loved me and how much he appreciated the financial help I provided. He ended his note with a mixture of Greek and Hebrew blessings.

Several months later, in early 1967, Goodyear transferred me to France to head the sales department. While Etty and our four daughters were sleeping on the plane, en route to Paris, I was awake, thinking about the challenges that my family and I would be facing in the new country. Nevertheless, there was a good side to our relocation to Paris, because it brought me closer to my siblings, to Tante Marie, and to my father in Israel. I remembered my father's face as he watched me eat the lunch he had prepared for me when I last saw him. I opened my wallet and again read his

Our family leaving Brazil for Paris in 1967; from left to right are Isabela, Claudia, Dora, and Marianne

card and his words of love and blessings. I slept for a while, my father's card still in my hand, until the squeal of the wheels landing on the runway awakened me.

As soon as we arrived at our hotel, the receptionist handed me two envelopes. One contained a welcome note from the CEO of Goodyear France—my new boss—and the other contained a telegram from Tel Aviv bearing devastating news. My father had died the day we were traveling to Paris. He had gone to the supermarket early that morning, a Friday, to buy a chicken and artichokes to cook for the weekend. He died from a massive heart attack as soon as he entered his house. The card that I had read again on the plane was a beautiful, symbolic way for him to say farewell to me.

I closed my eyes. I visualized him placing his hand over my head, the way he always did, and pronouncing the blessing that he had written on the card in a mixture of Hebrew and Greek.

I covered the card in plastic and kept it in my wallet for more than twelve years after my father's death. I read it thousands of times on my travels, mostly when I was alone on a plane or in my hotel room. Unfortunately, I lost it in Los Angeles when someone stole my briefcase. I still grieve its loss.

* * *

Goodyear France was suffering heavy losses, and the morale of the organization was desperately low. There, too, I rose up through the organization. By 1970, after my colleagues and I were able to improve not only our company's morale but also its financial performance, I had become the top executive at Goodyear France.

My next transfer was to corporate headquarters in Akron, where my family and I moved in 1974. I held a number of jobs in senior management until, in 1988, I reached the second-highest position in the company: that of president and chief operating officer for the worldwide tire business. I reported directly to the chairman and CEO, a man who had just been named to that position. But by that time, foreign tire companies with newly built facilities in the United States were giving us fierce competition. Tire companies everywhere were losing money, but because Goodyear is an American company it was subjected to much higher scrutiny and pressure from Wall Street.

All along, I was known as a man who relished challenges and was able to turn around difficult situations. This time, though, the corporate structure had to be changed at its roots and the sacred cows knocked down. I initiated my most extensive and daring restructuring plan, which involved all facets of our business. Many of these areas were fiercely protected by corporate officers.

In early 1991, in a desperate move, weighed down by his job's responsibilities and feeling that his days as chairman and CEO were numbered, my boss decided to eliminate my position in order to save his. But less than three months after my departure, the board of Goodyear decided to fire him anyway. One of the board members hastened to tell me, thinking that I would be glad to hear it and maybe even be willing to go back to Goodyear. This, however, was far from my mind. By that time, I wanted to give free rein to my management skills. I was determined to find companies I could run in my own style—companies I could put my own stamp on.

* * *

After leaving Goodyear I became sought after as an executive who could turn around financially troubled companies. These challenging jobs allowed me to achieve the kind of professional fulfillment I craved during my last years at Goodyear and at the same time attain the level of financial security I had been seeking since my adolescence in Egypt. I could never have achieved those goals had I remained at Goodyear.

From 1991 to 1997, I was CEO of a small corporation called Sudbury, Inc., based in Cleveland, Ohio. The company had filed for Chapter 11 bankruptcy protection, and my role was to save it from liquidation so that its creditors could recoup at least some of their losses.

When I met to discuss my employment agreement with representatives of the investment companies responsible for hiring me, I told them the salary was not important and that I would accept any figure they had in mind. They mentioned an amount less than half of what I was paid in my last job at Goodyear. To their surprise I accepted it without discussion. I said I was more interested in having equity in the reorganized company than I was in having a high salary. We were eventually able to settle on an equity stake that satisfied both them and me.

Sudbury—to which I commuted every day, a drive that took around thirty-five to forty minutes—occupied a whole floor of an office building. I dedicated my first week to meeting the staff, evaluating their capabilities, and understanding the businesses in which Sudbury was engaged at that time. Soon our head office became a buzzing beehive. Everyone knew what our objectives were and how we were going to attain them. I gave everyone the authority to accomplish his or her job. "Just do it" was something I said all the time. I could sense that people who had lost faith in the company—people in the head office and in the field—were starting to gain confidence. They were witnessing a different management style, one that was not willing to live with the status quo.

One day I went to the office, walked through the front door, and saw everyone standing up. I looked around. The walls were covered with large computer-printed banners and large cardboard letters that spelled out JUST DO IT! On the walls of the conference room the staff had added: WE DID IT, WE LIKED IT, LET'S DO IT AGAIN! I had a great feeling of satisfaction. I had a motivated office staff rallying behind me. And in August of 1992, just seven months after seeking court protection, Sudbury officially emerged from bankruptcy.

One event in particular stands out in my memory. Sudbury had been having a difficult relationship with the union that represented some of our employees. A meeting had been called to discuss terms for a new labor agreement. When I arrived, the union leader, a big, strong woman, was sitting at a large conference table, with union representatives on either side. Their faces were gloomy; they all had their arms crossed, signaling that they were entrenched in their position. The union leader stated in a firm tone that, unless we granted the concessions they were asking, they were ready to call a strike and shut down the plant.

I stood up and explained that Sudbury was coming out of bankruptcy and had strict commitments to the banks; it had to show continuous improvements in its financial performance. Failing to meet our commitments meant that the banks would liquidate our companies and that hundreds of people would lose their jobs.

I was still standing and talking when the union leader interrupted me. She wanted to know if we were ready to grant their demands. I did not answer. I sat down. I wanted to stop the discussion in order to dissipate the tension that had been building up. A long silence followed, during which I kept unconsciously rubbing the birthmark on my right wrist. This allowed me to discreetly look at my watch. "Yes, Mr. Sardas," the union leader said, breaking the silence. "Look at your watch—I bet it's a gold Rolex or one of those expensive executive watches." I did not say a word; I just took off the watch I was wearing and rolled it over the long conference table in her direction. It landed in her lap. She grabbed it, looked at it, and yelled, "Oh, my God, it's a cheap Timex!" She was laughing, and the whole group began laughing with her. The ice was broken.

We had a good exchange of points of view. When the union leaders realized that we could not go along with their demands, they switched the discussion to plant modernization and improvements in work conditions, a subject I was prepared to cover. The union leaders were impressed and asked to caucus in a separate office. When they came back, they were smiling, and they agreed to our proposal. The union leader came toward me and gave me a bear hug with her big, strong arms. We did not have any serious problems with the union after that meeting.

Sudbury's performance kept improving every month, far exceeding the market's expectations. My job was tough because it required traveling to remote locations, mostly to towns not served by commercial airlines. It was far from the lifestyle enjoyed by Goodyear executives. I did not ride in chauffeur-driven limousines or fly on company-owned airplanes. I didn't fly first class on commercial flights, nor did I stay in presidential suites at hotels. I often had to race through airport terminals with my much younger colleagues to catch our next flight. However, my job at Sudbury was heaven compared to the tense and frustrating environment I had faced during the last couple of years at Goodyear.

I enjoyed my job at Sudbury immensely because I was working with a group of young people who were diligent, skilled, and highly motivated. People often were surprised by my enthusiasm for a business whose sales were about 2 or 3 percent of Goodyear's. "How did you manage to adjust to such a significant disparity?" they would ask. The question often came from Wall Street investment bankers, and I would answer that when I looked at Sudbury's numbers, I just moved the decimal points. Because of Sudbury's situation, making a decision involving $100,000 was like making a $10 million decision at Goodyear.

I introduced a culture based on customer satisfaction; it emphasized quality, employee involvement at all levels, and continuous improvement. We established ambitious objectives while offering substantial rewards. We tied managers' compensation to the performance of each business unit and each business area. Good short-term results meant attractive bonuses. For long-term achievements employees were awarded equity participation in the form of stock options.

Both before and after filing for Chapter 11 protection, Sudbury was constantly in the news. I could not understand why it was attracting so much attention. Its size certainly did not justify it. Hardly a week passed without a large article about Sudbury in the *Cleveland Plain Dealer*, *Akron Beacon Journal*, or one of the area's many business magazines.

One article in particular attracted a lot of attention, not least because it was published by *Forbes*. The intention of the article was to provide hope to executives who had lost high-profile jobs in corporate America. It was entitled "Jack Likes the Test." The teaser above the title read, GETTING FIRED AT GOODYEAR WAS THE BEST THING THAT EVER HAPPENED TO IMMIGRANT JACK SARDAS—a statement that was totally true.

But it wasn't just journalists who were singing our praises. Even the banks that held our secured debt piled on the accolades. One banker told a reporter for *Crain's Cleveland Business*, in a story published on May 10, 1993, "This has probably been one of the most successful turnarounds that I've seen in my twenty years in banking."

* * *

In 1997, I became CEO of Dal-Tile International, located in Dallas, Texas, a company that had gone through a lengthy period of serious operational and financial problems. After a rapid review of Dal-Tile's businesses, I introduced an ambitious restructuring plan. I did not need too much time or many analytical studies; the experience I acquired in my previous jobs at Goodyear and Sudbury served me well. We ended up with a new organization that was more flexible and less costly. All our managers embraced the new structure and were extremely cooperative.

At Dal-Tile I introduced a culture that valued quality. During my talks and meetings, and in my writings, I established the objectives the company had to attain. I described and promoted the guiding principles I had in mind. I wanted a system based on teamwork and trust and on employee involvement at all levels. Dal-Tile was my baby, and I was going to shape its culture the way I had always wanted to shape the culture at Goodyear. I did not have to spend a lot of time or money to do it; I was going to teach the system to my executive and operating committees and enable them to teach their employees in turn. The culture was going to cascade from me to all levels of our company.

To strengthen Dal-Tile's foundation we asked every employee to establish objectives for their individual responsibilities that would help achieve corporate goals. This way, each of our employees knew what he or she had to accomplish to ensure that the company would have a long and successful future.

We created a trifold leaflet small enough to fit in a shirt pocket or a wallet; on it were printed Dal-Tile's corporate vision and its guiding principles and objectives. It also had space in which the department heads could outline their objectives and strategies and in which the employees could write down their own. Each employee received a leaflet. I was surprised but happy to learn that implementing a quality culture isn't terribly difficult; the employees welcomed it. Everything depended on the good faith of the head of the corporation. Soon the leaflet was the subject of conversation among all our employees, even the cleaning and maintenance personnel.

By the end of 1997 I had the reassuring feeling that our company was on the right track; we were all pulling together in the same direction with the same objectives. Dal-Tile had the right organization, the right processes, and the right culture. We were getting out of trouble and aiming at higher and broader horizons. We applauded and celebrated every success. High fives throughout Dal-Tile facilities were common practice. It was indeed enjoyable to watch our women and men high-fiving in the lobby and in meetings. Our new product presentations invariably provoked reactions of "Wow!" and "Oh!" We acknowledged individual efforts in our monthly and quarterly meetings. When we had a special job to accomplish, our managers often joined hands before leaving the office, as sports teams do before a match. We also had fun. Our meetings were engaging, efficient, and always focused on seeking further improvements, but humor was also present, even in the most serious sessions.

By 2001 all the financial analysts who covered building materials and construction products were praising Dal-Tile and saying that it was among the best companies in the industry. One sign that our success was at last being recognized was that we were being invited to conventions organized by major investment bankers for their most important industries. The building and construction products industry was given three or four such events every year.

At one of these events, I was impressed by the presentation given by Mohawk Industries, a family concern founded in upstate New York in 1878. It grew through a long series of mergers and acquisitions to become one of the top producers and sellers of carpet nationally. One day in early 2001, I got a call from Mohawk—the CEO and the CFO wanted to meet to discuss a merger. We sat down together in early October and, after long discussions and negotiations, we both agreed that the merger would be beneficial to both companies. After we arrived at a mutually acceptable price, and after we had obtained the approval of our respective boards, we announced the merger; it was completed in March of 2002.

I was happy to see that the merger had pleased all our constituents. Our employees, shareholders, and bankers did not stop thanking us for the value we had delivered. A large number of our employees became instant millionaires as a result of the transaction. Institutions and investment firms sent us congratulatory letters and expressed their gratitude. One such recognition appeared in June of 2002, in T. Rowe Price's semiannual report for its Small-Cap Value Fund; it made me feel happy and proud. It was written by the fund's portfolio manager and chairman of its advisory committee. He said:

> While most of the fund's holdings that are involved in takeovers produce satisfying gains, few merit comment in the shareholder letter. I want to depart from usual practice to publicly commend Dal-Tile International's CEO, Jacques Sardas, for his excellent stewardship in managing the company for the benefit of shareholders. We first met Mr. Sardas when he was a senior manager at Goodyear. Later, we invested in Sudbury—a troubled company that he revived—and earned a substantial profit for shareholders. Subsequently, when Mr. Sardas landed at Dal-Tile, we moved quickly to invest with him again, and again he delivered. If Jacques decides to come out of retirement, we hope he picks another small-cap public company for his "three-peat."

By that time our daughters had grown up and left the "nest," having started families of their own. Etty and I became comfortable in Dallas and have happily remained in that city, even after my tenure at Dal-Tile ended. I'm pleased and proud to say that I made many good friends among my colleagues at both Sudbury and Dal-Tile. Their hard work helped make the financial turnarounds possible.

* * *

Many people have asked me how I managed to live a successful life as a businessman and family man in spite of my humble beginnings. My answer is only four words long:

Our four daughters enjoy a moment together at sunset. From left are Dora, Claudia, Isabela, and Marianne.

determination and hard work. The world is full of highly educated people—many of them geniuses—who have failed because they lack determination and they don't work hard enough.

But there is another element that comes into play: luck. Luck smiles on those who drive themselves and are determined to succeed. I was lucky when I met and married Etty, my one and only love, my companion, my friend, my counselor, and my most dedicated supporter. In a way, this is her success story. She is the one who encouraged me when I was in doubt; she is the one who helped me overcome the most difficult challenges, and she's the one who took care of our four children and all our family concerns to allow me to fully concentrate on my work.

And I was lucky to have met and worked for Chuck Pilliod. He was the guardian angel who changed the course of my life and that of our entire family. We had no financial resources and were anxiously waiting for a miracle to happen. Chuck Pilliod was that miracle. He gave me an opportunity at Goodyear when I spoke little Portuguese and even less English. I had no professional skills and knew nothing about the tire and rubber business. Why did he hire me?

I asked myself that question many times since my first day at Goodyear, in 1957. I finally got the answer when Etty and I visited Chuck in a hospice in Akron in 2010. He was ninety-two years old and had lost his memory to Alzheimer's disease. His devoted wife, Nancy, had warned us that he no longer recognized his relatives and close friends. But when

Chuck Pilliod and I in 2010

we went to see him, he amazed us. He greeted Etty and me by name as soon as we walked in. After we spent a few pleasant hours together, I asked him a question that had intrigued me for many years. "Why did you hire me, Chuck?"

He thought for a minute, then he looked at me with a familiar grin. I knew he was about to make one of his infamous cutting remarks. "You know, everyone makes mistakes!" he said. This was the Chuck I'd always known, the Chuck of the good old times. But then he smiled, leaned over, and squeezed my arm. "Because you were a determined young man!" he added. It's true: when he interviewed me, he certainly saw not only a young, newly arrived immigrant desperately looking for an opportunity but also a young man fully determined to succeed. The words "without return" on my Egyptian exit visa had served as an incentive. They pushed me to work hard, so I did not have to look back with regret. Then I met Chuck, who believed in me and offered me the opportunity to succeed.

It struck me then that, in a way, our visit to Chuck was a kind of return. I needed to keep my friendship with him alive and to remember the many good years we spent together. They were formative years, just as my childhood years in Egypt were. After my visit to Chuck, I accepted the fundamental changes that had altered his body and mind, but they did not change what he meant to me. Maybe I could think of Egypt the same way. It, too, had gone through fundamental changes, but they shouldn't wipe away what the Egypt of my childhood meant to me. It was a beautiful country and had been an important part of my life.

Although the authorities in Egypt relaxed their strictures against admitting certain emigrants back within their borders in 1979, I never did return to the country of my birth. My siblings did, but I never had the opportunity or maybe even the desire to return. After my retirement, Etty and I were too busy traveling to other parts of the world, seeing new places and enjoying new experiences. So far, the words "without return" have been truly prophetic. And I'm proud to say that not returning was a choice—fully my own. But will I make another choice in the future? I don't know the answer.

EPILOGUE

I HAD LOST MY faith in God when I lost my mother, just as I was about to celebrate my tenth birthday. Losing my mother when I most needed her left a deep and permanent scar on my heart and soul. During the first few days after she died, people tried to console me by saying that it was God's will. I thought, *How could it be his will? How could I believe in a God who took the kindest and most dedicated mother away from her four children?* I became a rebel and continued to be a skeptic regarding religious matters when I grew up.

My bar mitzvah was part of our requirements at l'École Cattaui. We learned how to wear the tefillin one Thursday morning and had the bar mitzvah the following Saturday. All I had to do at the service was line up at the synagogue with seven or eight other thirteen-year-old boys—all, like me, from poor families. We had to wait our turn to recite the blessing of the Torah, consisting of two sentences, so that we could become a bar mitzvah. That was it.

I used to go to the synagogue when I was still in school just to be with my friends and make fun of them for their beliefs. While my friends were praying and showing off their ability to chant the prayers by heart, I was reading the French translations in the prayer books with a mixture of bitterness and skepticism, trying to collect enough ammunition to challenge what I believed was irrational in these books.

As an adult I retained my skepticism, but I stopped making sarcastic remarks when I left school and got busy with my work and my sports activities. I showed greater respect for our religion when I met and married Etty. This was more in deference to her and her family's religious devotion than in response to a change in my beliefs.

All along, deep in my heart, I was proud of being a Jew. I was not religious, but I was Jewish. I did not feel the need to go to the synagogue to pray and listen to sermons. I believed in kindness, justice, and fairness. I tried doing all the good I could do because doing it made me feel happy—not because I was looking for a divine reward. I avoided hurting people and committing evil actions—not because I was afraid I would be struck by a divine curse but because I thought that these actions were wrong. My pride in being Jewish meant that I fought back when anyone insulted our religion. When I was with our Maccabi basketball team, I played with all my heart because our team represented the Jewish community. I was proud of being Jewish when Israel was founded and later when it won the war against the surrounding Arab countries. I admired the Zionist leaders: Theodor Herzl, David Ben-Gurion, and Golda Meir. They were real leaders and visionaries. And if I could have, I would have fought for the creation of Israel when I was a teenager in Cairo.

When I grew older and was surrounded by my children and grandchildren, my skepticism toward my religion softened, in great part because of Etty's insistence. When we lived in Akron, she was an active member of the Beth El Congregation, and although I didn't attend services as frequently as she wished I did, I saw how much Jewish religious traditions meant to her. Among other things, I encouraged our family to attend and respect the Shabbat dinners on Friday evenings at our home, a tradition that I wanted my children and grandchildren to pass on. It's always a pleasure for me to watch the women and girls of our family lighting the Shabbat candles. It's a serene and solemn moment. Making a circle around the candles and covering their eyes with both hands, they recite the blessing in unison. The Shabbat dinners are especially important to Etty because

Four generations light Shabbat candles: from left to right are Bella, Etty's mother; Claudia holding her young daughter, Rachel; Etty, and Marianne

they also provide a reason for the family to gather at least once a week.

Another tradition we always observe is attending the service of prayer and repentance on Yom Kippur. Since I was ten years old I have never skipped fasting on that day, even when I happened to be on overseas assignments. The solemn and sacred atmosphere at the synagogue always moves me. The rabbis and the cantor are dressed in immaculate white robes and the large tallith they wear only on such special occasions. The synagogue's lights are bright, and people are quiet, respectful. The highly anticipated Kol Nidre, which means "all vows" in Aramaic, is recited before the evening service begins. The atmosphere becomes poignant and awe-inspiring as the cantor sings his melodious chants. I observe Yom Kippur not because I am afraid and want to atone for my sins but because I want to proclaim that I am a Jew.

Pesach—Passover—also moves me to strict observance. I have never eaten bread or any forbidden food during that week, even if my work took me to foreign countries. Why? Because throughout my life, the one consistent thing I could hold on to, besides the love and support of my family, was my identity as a Jew.

* * *

Such was my frame of mind when our youngest daughter, Claudia, who also lives in Dallas, asked me to accompany her and her son David to our synagogue, Congregation Shearith Israel, for a meeting in early 2010. Claudia wanted to discuss the arrangements she and her family were making for David's bar mitzvah with our cantor. After the meeting, as we were getting ready to leave, the cantor asked me, "Is it true that you'll be eighty this year?" He did not wait for my answer. "It will be a great mitzvah, a good deed, if you celebrate your second bar mitzvah with your grandson David."

I stood up and said, "Cantor, I have never read from the Torah, and I am not about to do it at my age." He smiled at me. "Try it—if you can't learn it, we'll find someone from the congregation who will replace you."

He opened a bound Torah on his desk and showed me the portion that was going to be read at David's bar mitzvah. "It's the section on Bamidbar [from the book of Numbers]. I could not find a short portion for you; they are all long, but I will help you." I did not say a word. Encouraged by my silence, the cantor went on: "Take this bound Torah with you so that you can start familiarizing yourself with it. Your portion will be Bamidbar Naso, chapter seven, verses twenty-four through thirty-five." I did not answer. Even though I was determined not to do it, I didn't want to spend time arguing. I took the book, shook his hand, and left with Claudia and David. There was nothing in the world that would force me to do what Claudia and the cantor had plotted.

When we got to our home, David, who had been quiet throughout the meeting at the synagogue, said to me, "Please, *please* have your bar mitzvah with me—it will really be cool."

My resolve began to erode, but I still did not want to give in. "David, I cannot read from the Torah. It's too difficult! I'm sorry, but I promise I'll make it up to you in other ways."

David put his arms around my shoulders. Staring at me with shining eyes, he said, "You always tell us that we can accomplish anything if we put our minds to it. This is very important to me. Please just put your mind to it."

His words decimated all my resistance. "I'll do it," I whispered. David and I embraced for a long time.

* * *

I had to start working on my Torah reading immediately; I had only a few weeks to learn what seemed like a huge number of difficult words. I picked up the bound Torah from the sofa and went to our bedroom, where I sat on the bed and meditated with the book on my lap.

Unlike many who read from the Torah without understanding it, I wanted to learn the meaning of each word in the verses assigned to me. The Hebrew verses were on the right-hand page, and their English translations were on the left. I turned to the beginning of the Bamidbar Naso section.

The first pages were about God asking Moses to take a census of the tribes assembled in the desert. God was giving precise instructions for counting the people in each tribe and assigning them specific tasks. The text went on to stipulate how to deal with a woman whose husband suspected she had "committed wrong." Then God explained how a Nazirite, a man who vowed to dedicate his life to God, had to behave. Samson was a Nazirite. As a young boy I admired his strength and was amazed by his exploits.

Memories of my childhood induced me into a long meditation. When I finally came back from my reverie, I took the bound Torah I was holding on my lap and tried to find the part that was assigned to me. Then my eyes landed on a verse that contains the blessings that God told Moses to ask Aaron and his sons to use when blessing the people of Israel. I was surprised to find them in the Torah. I thought they were the work of modern rabbis. I was not aware that these blessings, used every day in Jewish prayers, date back to the time of the Torah, around three thousand years ago. I had learned them by heart when I was a kid by listening to my father recite them so many times when blessing his children.

This was a great discovery and a magical moment for me. I read the blessings aloud, remembering my father holding the bag containing the tallith and tefillin and reciting those same blessings for each of his children while standing at the door to his bedroom, close to the mezuzah.

After reading the blessings from the Torah I was holding in my hands, I suddenly felt the urge to read the whole thing—the entire Pentateuch—even though I had only a short time to learn the portion I was to recite at David's bar mitzvah.

I read the book in the evenings, sometimes until dawn. I was impressed by what the Torah was revealing to me. Instead of searching for the absurd, I paid attention to the message, the philosophy, and the wisdom each passage conveyed. In the past I had focused on some unrealistic events just to exhibit my skepticism, to be cool. But I was looking at a few little trees and missing the huge forest.

The Torah is filled with laws, with lessons about determination and love. It exhorts us to be kind toward servants, hospitable to strangers, and compassionate to the poor. It impressed me with its sensible rules about discipline, health care, security, and, above all, respect for human beings and the holiness of life. Finally I understood the meaning of the word "heritage," so frequently used by our rabbis. Without the Torah I believe that Hebrew, the language spoken and written today in Israel and in many places all over the world, would have been a dead language, like Latin, ancient Greek,

Coptic, and Sanskrit. And, more important, Israel would not exist without the Torah.

My sarcasm and skepticism regarding the Torah had completely disappeared by the time I finished reading the last page. The reading did not turn me into a fervently religious Jew, but it did make me a better Jew.

The part I had to learn concerned offerings to God made by tribal chieftains. In the past I would have made some wise remark about these passages, but this was not the case anymore. I accepted that these events were related to a different world and occurred within a set of different conditions, norms, and expectations. I just had to respect these old practices and start learning how to sing the verses in accordance with the rules of the Torah.

* * *

The moment of truth came on Saturday morning, May 22, 2010. David performed with impeccable assurance. When my turn came, I went slowly to the bimah, the platform where I had to stand facing the congregants. The cantor was standing there with another man, who was holding a bound Torah. This man was there to carefully follow my reading and make sure I sang my verses with the right melodies and with no mistakes; if I made a mistake, he would interrupt me to correct me. Mistakes in reading the Torah are not allowed.

I sang the blessing with a firm voice, and everything went well from there on. I did not hesitate, and I did not misread or sing a wrong note. I was not interrupted, meaning that my reading was correct.

When I finished, I looked out at the congregants in attendance at the synagogue that Saturday morning. I recognized many familiar faces. I saw some of my former coworkers; I saw friends from our Jewish federation and our Jewish community center. I saw people who had come from many parts of the world to be with me on this important occasion.

And then I looked at the seats close to the bimah, where I was standing, and I saw the people who mean more to me than anything else in the world. I saw my wife, Etty, the love of my life, who supported me and inspired me and with whom I had shared fifty-four years of hopes and dreams. I saw our daughters and their husbands and their children. Their smiles, their ebullience—their joie de vivre—filled my heart with pride and happiness.

* * *

With David at our bar mitzvah

I started writing this book a few years ago. To see it come to fruition feels more important and gratifying than any of my professional successes. I wrote it for my family, particularly for my grandchildren. Their questions and curiosity inspired me. My story, after all, is part of theirs. As they get older, I hope they will continue to be curious—that they, too, will ask questions, seek knowledge, and pass along their stories to their children and grandchildren. I hope this book will inspire them as they have inspired me.

I also have to admit that I wrote this book with the hope that it would encourage others—parents and grandparents—to write down their stories and keep the torch of family history burning from generation to generation. After all, as Jews, it is our custom to keep stories going, to keep traditions alive, for those who come after us. There are some things we must never forget. One of the most powerful is the story of the Exodus, which we recite every year through the Passover Haggadah, the narrative of the Jewish escape from Egypt. As slaves, the ancient Jews were persecuted and oppressed. They fled Egypt, seeking freedom in an unknown land. The story is relived during the Passover seder, when all members of the family are united at the table. Children play an important role by asking four questions. The eldest among us are always eager to hear the youngest ask: "What makes this night different from all other nights?" We then take pleasure in answering the question the way we—and our forebears—have done for generations.

My family's departure from Egypt—with no return—was also an exodus. As our ancestors did, we left everything behind to flee persecution and oppression. The only things we kept were our memories. I'm sure the ancient Jews felt the same anxiety and sadness we felt when we left the place that had captured our hearts and souls. But in the end, just as we did, they chose freedom over the ephemeral comfort of a painful, dangerous, and degrading life.

Rituals such as the Passover seder and the bar mitzvah originated in ancient times. If each generation did not take seriously its responsibility to pass along its traditions and stories to those who follow, where would we be? It is in that spirit that I offer this tale of a young man, born and raised in Egypt, whose first bar mitzvah in Cairo was suffused with gloom, uncertainty, and despair and whose second bar mitzvah, in his eightieth year, was suffused with happiness, safety, and hope.

ACKNOWLEDGMENTS

I NEVER IMAGINED THAT bringing a book to fruition would be one of the toughest tasks I would face in my life. The writing was just the tip of the iceberg—the beginning of a much more complex process. Many people helped me along the way.

First, thank you to Barbara Clark, who took charge of the editing and many other tasks. She handled every phase of the process, every challenge, with aplomb. Barbara is not only our editor but also our friend.

Thank you also to our talented book designer, Patrice Sheridan, and our eagle-eyed proofreader, Pat Jalbert-Levine.

I am particularly thankful to our close longtime friends Sam and Salma Gibara, who over the course of many years became part of our family and a reliable source of wisdom and support. They read the manuscript when it was still in its infancy and encouraged me to persevere.

There is no way I could have started—much less finished—my book if it were not for the prodding and sometimes even harassment that came from my family. A special thank you to our daughters, Dora, Marianne, Isabela, and Claudia, who read the manuscript in its initial phase and told me that it was a page-turner, a term I found quite generous.

Thank you also to my cousin Denisica Lévi. We consider her our sister, as she was an integral part of our childhood. She has an amazing, sharp memory, and she provided valuable information about dates and names when I needed them. She also lent me many old pictures.

My siblings, Léon, Saby, and Denise, played an important role in my life. During our frequent reunions in Tel Aviv, we used to enjoy reliving the fun as well as the sad moments from our younger years in Egypt. Our reminiscences helped me when my memory failed. Léon, Saby, and Denise also provided me with valuable family pictures that I hadn't seen before. They followed the progress of my book and urged me to persist not only with gentle reminders but also with pranks and sharp teasing, mostly from Léon. He died the evening of December 17, 2014, a day after his ninety-first birthday. Saby, Denise, and I were at his bedside, and his eyes twinkled with mischief when he was telling us his jokes, his last jokes! His irrepressible personality filled our lives with laughter and joy. We miss him terribly.

Finally, my deepest thanks go to my wife, Etty, who patiently endured the many months of writing, rewriting, and hand-wringing that accompanied the publication process. She also encouraged me to keep going on the many occasions when I felt like giving up. For this and so much more, she is the book's true hero.